"'Naked Glass' is a subtle, poignant story whose narrator's desire to temper honesty with love, ordinariness with beauty, transforms her sighting of two human bodies into a finely nuanced insight into the human heart."
– Robert Olen Butler, winner of the Pulitzer Prize for Fiction

On "The Salvation of My Soul": "A beautifully crafted, deeply moving, nearly visionary piece of work...you are clearly a remarkably talented woman."
– Steve Stern, author of *The Angel of Forgetfulness*

On "To This Day": "Very strong, energetic, well written. Quite terrific, an accomplished piece of writing."
– Mikhail Iossel, National Endowment for the Arts and Guggenheim Fellowship award winning author

Stories from the Middle of Nowhere

Susi

Klare

Stories From the Middle of Nowhere
First Edition

Paperback ISBN: 978-1-945587-51-1
Library of Congress Control Number: 2020906060

Susi Klare
Stories From the Middle of Nowhere
1. Literary Fiction; 2. The West; 3. Landscape; 4. Oregon
Book Design: Dancing Moon Press
Cover photograph: Dominic DeFazio
Dancing Moon Press
Bend, Oregon USA
dancingmoonpress.com

PRIOR PUBLICATIONS

"As if Keeping it Secret" originally published in *Peregrine* 2000 under the title "Choices." Also published online in *WIN Magazine*, 2001

"At the Intersection of Heaven and Hell" originally published in *Fish Anthology* 2005. Also published in *Gargoyle*, 2008

"Dalai Lama" originally published in *Mississippi Review*, 2005 Prize Issue

"Grizzly Moon" originally published in *Explorations* 2000

"The Salvation of My Soul" originally published in *River City* 2004

"Naked Glass" originally published in *The Best of Carve Magazine*, Volume 4. Also published in *High Desert Journal*, 2005 fall issue.

"The Possibility of Wolves" originally published in *Fish Anthology* 2005 under the title "The Logger"

"Cosmo" originally published in *Inkwell*, Spring 2007

"Things Could Go Either Way" originally published in *Dogwood*, 2005

"To this Day" originally published in *Other Voices* 40

In loving memory of Dominic DeFazio,
who made everything possible

"Fiction is the lie through which we tell the truth." —Albert Camus

Contents

As If Keeping It Secret

We're in the kitchen washing the supper dishes when Amber asks me if I've ever had an abortion. My hands stop still in the soapy water and I give my daughter a raised eyebrow look.

"No, I'm not pregnant!" she snaps. Then slams the plate she's rinsing alongside the others on the dish rack. The tone of her voice, this tone that Amber reserves just for me, it makes my eyes go searching outside the window, out there in the rain. But it's too dark to see into the forest. There's only our double-glazed reflection, the two of us standing at the sink, shoulder to shoulder, each of us wearing a ghost double a few inches off to the side. Windblown rain slices across the glass. And I tell myself for the thousandth time, things shouldn't feel like this between a mother and her child.

But then, I suspect that Amber's been mad at me from day one.

I take my hands out of the warm dishwater. "Leave the rest," I say. "I'll finish later." I ask Amber to please come with me into the study. She blows the bangs off her forehead, and I know I'm not supposed to take all these little putdowns so personally, I know it's just an age, but I also know something else. I know why this girl has every right to be mad at me. I know what it is that haunts her soul.

Amber follows me through the empty house. Her father and her brother have gone to town for basketball practice at the middle school, and for the next couple of hours we have the place to ourselves. I go to my desk in the study and open a drawer. Under a pile of old letters I find a worn envelope. I take the envelope to the sofa and I sit down. Amber stays standing there in the doorway, barefoot, in her tank top and shorts, as if we weren't in the middle of our cold wet winter. She leans one hip into the doorframe and crosses her arms over her chest. I pat the cushion beside me and ask her to come sit with me. She stands in the doorway a moment longer, lets loose a weary sigh, then comes to the sofa and perches herself on the far edge.

Everything, everything this girl does in my presence is an accusation.

Inside the envelope is a small black and white photograph. I take the photo out, touching only its white edge, then turn and hand it to my daughter. She grabs it between her thumb and forefinger and I have to bite my lip to keep from telling her to get her thumb off the print. She looks from the photo to my face, then back again at the photo. She can't believe it's me.

"You were gorgeous," she says. "And your hair, when did you cut it off?"

"A few months after that picture," I say, and I can still see the long tendrils falling around my feet in the jungle mud. It was dusk, and the last of the day's light seemed to luminesce from the growing pile of hair. Blonde was such a wrong color in that green land of dark-skinned people. I wanted to kick leaves over it, but Leanne told me to stand still, she was having enough trouble cutting through the thick stuff with the dull scissors on her Swiss army knife. Leanne yanked at my hair and I kept my eyes aimed at the ground and I listened to the parrots, large flocks of them passing overhead on their way home to roost, their screeching cries, the rush of all those wings. Still, it wasn't enough to drown out the choking sounds Leanne was making, my best friend trying not to cry out loud, both of us wanting only to be invisible.

"If I had hair like that, I'd keep it," Amber says. "And who's the guy with the eyes?" She holds the picture closer to her face.

"His name was Juan Carlos," I say.

Amber nails me with one of her looks and there's no turning back now. No choice but to finish what I've started.

"That's our wedding picture," I say.

Amber slaps the photo down on the coffee table.

"Please!" I say. I try to make my voice calm. "Please don't put your hand all over it like that, I've already lost the negative."

"You never told me," Amber says, her eyes full of blame. As if *this* were the betrayal.

And for a small moment I'm tempted to laugh at my daughter. With all her posturing, how little this girl really knows. But I shake off the impulse. I close my eyes and I rub two fingers into the creases over the bridge of my nose. How can I explain to Amber that I didn't know I was getting married? I hardly spoke Spanish, much less the *Quiché* language of the Indians. Back then, it was all about going with the flow—throw a few things into a pack, point your thumb south, and one day you and Leanne find yourselves in Guatemala eating magic mushrooms with the natives. Is a girl supposed to hear such things from her mother?

"Did you love him more than Daddy?" Amber says.

The weight of my head presses into my fingers and here is Juan Carlos, stepping from the narrow black doorway of his mother's house. Juan Carlos in the bright sunlight, his cotton pants so white against his brown skin. Juan Carlos watching me pass on the dusty street, the delight of a child in his face, his face so smooth and guileless it made my breasts ache. And that machete he always wore at his hip, how it somehow led me to imagine his hands on my body.

I straighten my spine. Drop my hands to my lap and open my eyes. "Love can't be quantified," I say, and of course these words are a mistake. My chest tightens as Amber gives me one of her looks and it doesn't help to argue with myself that this is just an age, this is hormones, this is not about me.

"Daddy is the one I'm sharing my life with," I say. "Daddy is the one I've had my babies with." Sweat is drenching my armpits, but the hands that grip each other in my lap are cold. Amber looks at me with ice in her eyes, her eyes calling me a liar. But all I can do is go on and on with words and words and words. Words about Amber's father, and they are all good words. Words like *appreciate* and *grateful* and *admire*. I want my daughter to see how lucky we are to have a good man to take care of us. Just think, we could have ended up like Leanne and her fatherless children, it happens to so many women, the wrong men they choose.

Amber is slumped back on the sofa, her arms again folded tight across her chest. She interrupts my speech and says to the ceiling, "Why are you talking about Leanne and her loser boyfriends? Why can't you just answer a question?

Why do you have to turn everything into a teaching moment?" That voice again, that tone that would have earned me a slap across the face from my mother.

"Amber," I say.

"What?"

"Nothing."

I've only slapped Amber's face once, and that was when she was five and purposefully threw a bowl of oatmeal to the floor. Waste is the one sin in my household. It doesn't matter that we have plenty, I can't forget how there was never enough to eat in that Guatemalan village, how I helped myself to what I wanted, the tortillas I took whenever the basket was offered.

"All I'm asking," Amber says, "is was this guy your… One. True. Love?" She shapes the words with her mouth as if speaking to someone who's deaf.

"I was young," I say.

"Never mind," she says.

"What can a girl that age know about love?" I say.

"I *said*, never mind."

"One thing I can tell you," I say, "is that those were the sweetest people you'd ever want to meet. Such a relief after Texas and Mexico. We hitched, if you can believe that. I hesitate to tell you, I don't want to give you ideas. Hitching is so dangerous these days, with all the psychopaths and—"

Amber cuts me off with a raised hand.

"In any event, it was a different world in the sixties," I say. "Of course, men will be men."

"What's that supposed to mean?" Amber says. "Did you and Leanne get raped?"

"We were lucky not to," I say. "I don't know what was worse, the Texans with their sneaky eyes whenever they thought we weren't watching, or those Mexicans, how their eyes crept slow and naked over our bodies."

"Gross," Amber says. But her eyes are eager and she turns her body to face me.

"I'm sorry," I say. "I shouldn't be talking to you this way. I want you to know it was only *certain* men, we don't ever want to judge a culture by the behavior of a few men."

Amber rolls her eyes to the ceiling.

"In any event," I say, "things mellowed out as we went farther south, and then one day Leanne and I found ourselves in a different world. We were in Guatemala."

"That's where you met *him*?" Amber says. "In Guatemala?" She leans toward the coffee table. With exaggerated care she uses one fingernail to edge the photograph over the lip of the table, then drops it onto the palm of her other hand. She lifts her palm and looks at the picture again. "He's got a familiar face," she says.

I have to remind myself to breathe. I turn my head from side to side, loosen my neck. I must speak carefully now, must not turn my daughter away from what she is about to know.

"A familiar face?" I say. "What makes you say that?"

"It's *so* National Geographic," she says. Her words are weightless, dismissive.

"Meaning...?" I say.

"You know what I mean," Amber says. "Anyway, I can see why you fell in love with him. Who wouldn't?" She reaches out her arm and drops the photo on my lap, then lifts herself off the sofa, and for a moment it seems that she's about to leave the room, but all she does is pull her naked legs up under her. She twists her body and flings one arm over the back of the sofa and now she's facing me full on and

I must find my way through the rest of the story.

"I know you'll think what I did was no more than a cheap self-indulgence," I say. "And yes, I did what I did with a young man I couldn't even talk to. But for *that*, you don't need words." I gaze down at the picture of myself and Juan Carlos. My mouth shapes itself into a small smile and I look up from the photo, but Amber is not about to be my girlfriend in this.

I lower my eyes again. Of course. My daughter will see what I did. How I came into that land, no different than the *Conquistadores* before me. How I took what I wanted.

"In any event," I say, "it all ended."

"How come?" Amber says.

"Oh Amber," I say, "there were so many endings. There was the baby. There was Juan Carlos. There was the village. There were the four hundred and thirty-nine other villages." And I look into my daughter's face and I ask her, "Which ending do you want me to start with?"

"You had a baby?"

"No," I say. "I went to the *curandera*…"

"The *what*?"

"The medicine woman," I say. "Only I did this in a neighboring village, because by the time I figured out I was pregnant, I knew enough to hide what I was doing from Juan Carlos."

"Your husband," Amber says.

"That's what *he* thought," I say, "and I guess the rest of the village thought that too. I suppose I should have known from how happy he was that he'd gotten me pregnant, and for awhile, I almost believed it myself, that a baby could be something to be happy about. I told myself I was part of the community. I wore my hair in braids, I ran around the village in a long skirt and a bright red *huipil*, and even though the women still giggled and touched my hair, they were also teaching me how to weave the village pattern. You know, every village, has their own woven pattern and in this village—"

"You had an abortion?"

"I'm sorry," I say, "but I'm trying to tell you what it was like in that place. How lost I was in the dream, how in my dream these people had no word for *uptight* and no language for things like *worry* or *dread*. How wrong I was, how dead wrong. How I didn't know anything about what went on behind those dark eyes." I try to see into my daughter's eyes. They've always been a much deeper blue than mine, not nearly as transparent. "Can you just let me do this?" I say.

Amber sits still and gives me the slightest nod, so I go on. Quick, before she changes her mind and hits me with more attitude.

"Then one day I saw this soldier standing at the edge of the jungle. This soldier in a dark green uniform and he would *not* smile at me. I almost laughed, the first time I saw him, how he had his cap pulled down so tight it hid his eyes, how he acted so dead serious, so opposite from the *campesinos* in their loose straw hats, always free and easy with their smiles. He was just a boy, really, but there was something about how he held his rifle across his chest, I had to look away. And soon there were others, more soldiers like him hanging out at the edge of town, and I noticed that the women didn't giggle as much as they used to. They still whispered into each other's ears, but now they whispered words like *prisión, militar, helicoptero*."

Amber is finally here now. My daughter is finally here with me, a daughter who sits still and listens to her mother's words.

"I woke up from the dream," I say. "I woke up from the dream and admitted that I was just another tourist on vacation."

"Is that when you had the abortion?" Amber says. "Did it hurt?"

"No, it wasn't that kind of abortion," I say. "It was all done with herbs. Some bitter tea I had to drink several times a day. It was really no big deal."

Amber pulls her head back a notch.

"The *tea,*" I say. "Its *taste* wasn't so bad. Of course, ending a life…" I search Amber's face. I search to see if she will recognize what it is that haunts us both.

I go on. "By then I'd heard from Leanne that the men were meeting in secret at night. Leanne was sleeping in her tent at the edge of the village, not that she had to, any one of those families would have fed her their last chicken to have her as a houseguest, but you know Leanne. Even after the soldiers showed up, Leanne said if she could handle the snakes she could handle the soldiers."

I stop talking. Before my mouth can veer off into one of Leanne's snake stories, my fingers come to my lips, cold against the warm of my mouth. I lower my hand back to my lap and bring myself back to the story that needs telling. Amber sits still, she is waiting for me to go on.

"So anyway, one night I woke up feeling nauseous and Juan Carlos was gone. I went outside to throw up and I saw all these shadowy shapes. It was the men of the village sneaking back into their houses. And I went back to bed and I waited and when Juan Carlos finally came in he started yelling a bunch of stuff in Spanish and *Quiché*. I understood the word *curandera* and that's when I knew that the gossip had reached our village. He started ransacking the room until he found where I'd hidden the cloth bag with the herbs. I think he wanted to hit me. I told him I had to get back to school. *Escuela*. That was one of the words they all understood. His eyes got like the soldier's. He said something in *Quiché*, then he said '*Yo soy muerto*.'"

"I am dead?" Amber says.

"Those were the last words I heard from Juan Carlos. He went into the jungle and committed suicide."

"He killed himself?" Amber says.

I close my eyes and all I can do is nod my head, just the slightest movement up and down. I will not tell my daughter how, in my mind's eye, he did this terrible thing at the exact moment, the exact moment I was spreading my feet in the mud and lifting my skirt to squat, to pass something I refused to look at, or maybe did look at and only now refuse to remember. I will not tell my daughter how sometimes I see him do it with the machete he always wore at his hip, or how at other times I see him do it with herbs, herbs more sudden and powerful than the ones I took, some bitter sap from a tree or maybe psilocybin mushrooms. Juan Carlos on his knees in the jungle and I can still feel his tongue turn numb, while I squat in another part of the jungle and I bite my lower lip until it bleeds. How I still feel the constriction in his throat until he can no longer swallow, the taste of blood in my mouth, how we both lift our faces to the blurring canopy, both hear the muffled cries of the parrots flying home to roost, the fading rush of their wings.

"How?" says Amber's voice. "How did he do it?"

I lift and drop my shoulders. "Who knows?" I say. "Leanne and I weren't invited to the funeral. No one would speak to us." I'm rubbing my eyebrows with my cold fingers, not yet ready to look at my daughter, not yet ready to see what she may understand of this story.

The room is silent but for the sound of rain on the roof. I feel Amber waiting. I open my eyes, and yes, Amber is still with me, still waiting for more.

"I never even knew if it was really me he wanted or just his dark fingers in my *gringa* hair," I say. The room blurs and I can still shiver at the feel of his fingers stroking my hair, my downcast eyes on the sharp blade of the machete on his hip.

I look up and sharpen my eyes on my daughter. "In any event," I say. "I never meant to shame him. How could I have known?"

Amber takes the picture in her hands. Traces a circle around the two faces there, running her finger across its surface.

"Please be careful with that," I say and immediately regret my words. Always my stupid careless words. And now Amber carefully puts down the photo, then goes into a huddle at the far end of the couch, her arms wrapped around her legs, her legs drawn to her chest. She stares over my left shoulder.

Amber is again lost to me.

"Baby?" I say. I reach across the distance between us to touch her arm. Her flesh is warm against my cold fingertips. "Will you forgive me?"

"For what?" Amber says. "I never even knew the guy. And as for that other thing, you know I'm pro-choice."

She looks down at my fingers on her arm until I take them back. And now I see her tears, but Amber never cries any more. The water swells in her eyes, does not flow, only evaporates like the moisture that sizzles to the surface when you burn green wood.

"I don't know why I'm weirding out over this," Amber says. "It's not even like there was a *baby* involved, it was just a fetus." She puts her fists in her eyes, then her feet on the floor. She's about to get up and leave.

"No, wait!" I say. It's all I can do not to reach over and hold her in place. Not to cry out to my daughter, *please don't leave me again.*

"I always knew it was you," I say.

"What?" Amber says.

And now the words rush out of my mouth like jungle ants from a burning log. "Every morning when I was pregnant with you I'd wake up with this question, *who is the father of this baby?* And of course your dad was the only man I'd been with for years, but still, almost every morning for nine months, I'd lie in bed next to Richard and have to work through this tangle inside my head, because they were both there inside me, Richard and Juan Carlos, and each one of them was claiming you as his. So every morning I had to remind myself that Juan Carlos had been dead for over ten years and even if that *was* my fault he would have been killed by the soldiers or the flames or the helicopters, all the men were, and if I'd kept you then you wouldn't have had a father."

Amber stares past me, her gaze fixed on the window behind my left shoulder, the deep wet forest out there, hidden in darkness. She hugs her knees to her chest.

"I'm sorry if I hurt you," I say. "I'm sorry I couldn't let you through the first time, but it's better for you here, better in *this* forest, better with *this* family, can't you see that?"

Amber says nothing. Amber sees nothing, her eyes off over my left shoulder. No, Amber sees everything.

"Amber?" I say. "That village was no place for a baby." I lean toward my daughter and I whisper the name of the village. I whisper the name, as if keeping it secret could change what happened. As if keeping it secret could hide it from the helicopters, could hide it from everything that happened.

The Possibility of Wolves

I get woke up too early by someone running a chainsaw. Joey's asleep next to me, and from how his breathing never changes, I can tell he doesn't hear a thing – this is a guy who brags how he slept through it when Mount Saint Helens blew up. I want to hide my ears under his armpit, but he clamps his arm to his ribs like I'm trying to trespass his private property.

The chainsaw goes on and on and on, until it just about puts me back to sleep. Then it stops. I lay there and listen – clink, clink, clink – while someone pounds a metal wedge into the cut. It goes in between my ribs, right into my chest, till red blood spurts from my heart. Joey would say that's a pretty stupid way to see things, but I can't help it. I don't paint the pictures in my head.

Joey was a lot nicer before he got laid off at the sawmill.

The hammering stops and it gets quiet as all death. Until that last spine of wood holding up the tree starts to crackle apart, thread by thread. The trailer goes trembly, and then BOOM! The noise hits my bones. It wakes Joey enough so he pushes me over and starts to noodle around my rear. Joey always says what a great ass I have, but I wish he wouldn't. When he talks like that it makes me want Mama here in this trailer instead of him.

The chainsaw starts again, and I turn to wake Joey the rest of the way up. "Joey!" I say. "They're cutting down the last good place."

Joey tells me to hush up. He still won't open his eyes. If Joey really loved me like he said when he first moved in, you'd think he'd try once in a while to feel what I feel. He wouldn't act so smart every time I say something about them cutting down all the trees. He wouldn't walk around Mama's trailer and smack his hand up against every chair and cupboard and say, "What do you think *this* is made from?"

The rain on the roof is a thousand chickens pecking on a thousand tin drums. I wish it would rain harder, hard enough to drown that chainsaw. Hard enough to make the logger go home.

Joey rolls me to my back. He gets on top and uses his hand to cram in his thing. It's not the first time, but it still feels like getting torn open. Only for a minute though. And now Joey's sweating so hard he forgets I'm here, which gives me a chance to think if there's anything I can do about the logger. Like go over there with Joey's shotgun and shoot over his head. But that might bring the sheriff, which is the absolute last thing I can afford to have happen. Or I could try and talk him into leaving. If he's not too old, I might even find us a dry spot – you can always find something if you know where to look – and let him do what Joey's doing.

I can't help it, I don't paint the pictures.

It's not so bad, if you can get over the first part. I could keep that logger busy in the moss, and if he's anything like Joey, he'd fall asleep and forget about me once he was done. That's when I'd run off with his chainsaw. I'd throw it in the river.

It's not the worst thing in the world, what Joey's doing. I start to wiggle around under him, until he makes a noise like a dog when you step on its tail, then collapses on my chest. Now Joey's warmer than a blanket. I could stay buried here forever. But he rolls off and goes back to sleep. That leaves nothing but empty cold air hitting my skin where he sweated all over me. I cover us back up and try to keep it quiet, with my face squished into his back. Joey wakes up and says, "What're you crying about?"

"Nothing," I say.

"Well, you got my back wet," Joey says. "That's not nothing."

Outside, the chainsaw revs up harder, then stops.

Joey slaps off the covers and gets up. He pulls up his jeans and puts socks and T-shirts in a duffel bag. I never noticed how cramped Mama's trailer was until Joey moved in. That's how big he is. Not exactly fat, it's mostly muscles from working at the mill. I watch his muscles move under the white skin on his back. I wish he'd come back to bed for awhile. But then another tree falls. And even though it's across the way, the noise and shaking are like it's all happening right inside Mama's trailer.

"Joey?" I say.

"The mill's done for," Joey says, not looking up from his duffel. "I gotta go to town for a few days. I gotta find something else." He zippers shut the duffel.

That zipper bothers my ears as bad as the chainsaw.

***

The porch is cold and slimy under my feet. I wave at Joey's jeep, until all that's left is tailpipe smoke and the faded sound of shifting gears. The rain is gone for now. Quiet sunshine lights the treetops on the hill across the way. Then clink, clink, clink, and one treetop moves its arms like someone about to drown. Then it goes under.

You can hear things breaking all the way down.

***

The new thistles in the pasture are stuck flat to the ground like spiky gray snowflakes, and the stinging nettles are almost a foot high. The thistles are the worst to step on, sharp as needles, and I remember how me and Mama used to make a game out of crossing the pasture barefoot. This time I'm carrying a brown paper sack in front of my chest, which makes it harder to see where I'm stepping. The brown paper sack is full of temptations.

Everywhere you look dead things leftover from winter are getting buried under fresh green. I stop on the bridge and rest the sack on the rail. The fish that are supposed to be in the river aren't. I give up looking and head up into the forest. I just follow the noise.

***

The logger doesn't see me. He's down on one knee pouring gas into his chainsaw from a red can with a bent silver nozzle. He's got on a yellow hard hat, and the rest of his face is hid under a dark beard.

Already I don't recognize the place, with sunshine blasting in where it's always been green light and cool shadows. It looks like I'm too late, everything's already torn to hell. Fallen tree trunks, branches broken every which way, all the trilliums with their petals limp and twisted from getting caught in the sun.

He looks over and sees me. I stand there with my toes curled into the wet moss, the sun hot on my neck, steam coming off everything, the smell of sap and sawdust and gas. The logger gets up and wipes his hands on his legs. He's got on a gray wool jacket over greasy pants, the hard-hat shading his eyes.

I'm the one supposed to say something. "Could I please ask you to stop?" I say. I hug the paper sack tight to my chest.

"Excuse me?" the logger says. He takes off his yellow hard hat and sets it on a fresh stump. His hair is smushed wet underneath, it's as dark as his beard and tied back in a frizzy ponytail.

"Would you mind not cutting down any more trees?" I say.

Sparkles of sap have oozed out the top of the stump. The sap doesn't know yet that it's got nowhere to rise.

"You must be a tree hugger," the logger says.

"I never hugged a tree unless I was up in it," I say, "and that's just to keep from falling when the wind kicks up." Just then the bottom of the sack tears and everything falls out. A Budweiser can hits sharp across the top of my foot, but I don't let on how bad it hurts. I drop to my knees and start picking up cans of beer and broken chocolate chip cookies. I'm busy loading everything into the front of Mama's white peasant blouse, which I probably shouldn't be wearing, when I feel from the change in the light that the logger is standing over me.

"How come you're not in school?" says his voice from on high. The round steel toe of his boot appears beneath my face and nudges a Budweiser.

My fingers go deep in the moss. If you were a bug you'd

see how the moss makes a forest you could hide in, every piece of moss built like a fern, a whole forest of giant ferns.

"I quit," I say. "I quit school when Mama's cancer got terminal."

His knee comes down and sinks in the moss, and he picks up a ziplock bag. The cracks in his fingers are just as black as under his nails.

"That's the last of Mama's salmon jerky," I say. I grab the ziplock from his hand and stuff it into Mama's peasant blouse, along with everything else. "It's not hatchery fish," I say. "They're wild Chinook."

You can hear the river off in the distance. If you didn't know it was a river, you'd think it was just wind in the trees. The air is full of the smell of trees dying. Nothing like how people smell when they die.

***

I'm on the logger's gray wool jacket, which he put over the ground for me to sit on, just like they do in the movies. Then he sat himself in the wet moss facing me. He's got on rainbow-colored suspenders over a white T-shirt that's torn at the collar. We're eating chocolate chip cookies.

"I got the recipe off the bag of chocolate chips," I say.

"Yum," the logger says. He closes his eyes to taste how good they are. He's got eyelashes as dark and pretty as Deedee Lamont's.

"I shouldn't be working anyway," he says. "The guy who's supposed to cut with me never showed up this morning." He pulls the tab off a Budweiser. "It's against company policy to cut by yourself." The beer spits foam all over his dirty fingers. He lifts the dripping can toward one of the trees he already cut. "Especially when they're this big," he says. Even fallen flat on its back, the trunk makes a high wall through the woods. The logger hands the beer over to me, like he thinks I might want some.

"You already tore everything to hell," I say. I take a drink from the can. I try not to make a face at how awful beer tastes.

"If not me, it would just be someone else," he says. He picks up another beer. His arm doesn't look as strong as Joey's, but strong enough. His chainsaw is bright orange behind him. It looks big to run with, the business end about as long as me. The logger sees me eyeballing his chainsaw. "You can't stop these things," he says. He finishes his beer, easy as water, and starts in on another one.

We sit quiet and drink our beers while the damp seeps up through his gray wool jacket and into my pants.

***

"You want some more chocolate chip cookies?" I lift the bottom of Mama's white peasant blouse from my lap and show what's left. Mostly just broken pieces and crumbs. I hope bleach works on chocolate stains.

"I think I'll pass," he says. "I'm not sure it's a good idea to mix sweets with beer." He's got eyes like river rocks, how you see their color when the sun's on the water.

"You should try some of this," I say. I get a piece of Mama's salmon jerky from the ziplock. "This fish probably swam all the way to Alaska and back," I say.

The logger chews and chews and chews. If he wanted to kiss me, his mouth would taste like salt. My eyes go down to his chest.

"Where'd you find rainbow-colored suspenders?"

He pops one with his thumb. "Present from a friend."

"Your girlfriend?"

He tips back his head and drinks down his Budweiser.

He's got beard hairs on his adam's apple.

"I'll bet your butt's all soaked by now," I say. "Mine is, and I'm on your jacket."

"No matter," he says. "When you work in the woods you're always wet from either rain or sweat. Usually both."

"You could find another job," I say.

He turns the empty can between his knees like he's reading the small print. "Maybe," he says. "I suppose I could work on a fishing boat. I've been meaning to get up to Alaska one of these days."

"The furthest I've been is Cannon Beach," I say. "But I have a book that occurs in Alaska. It's called *Julie of the Wolves,* about a girl who runs away from home after her mother dies." My hand makes a fist around the beer can. The can pops loud enough to drive off every wild animal for a mile around.

"She gets adopted by wolves," I say. "I read it twice, once to myself and once out loud to Mama, but the second time I didn't get all the way to the end." I bite the edge of the can till it hurts my teeth.

"From what I hear, Alaska's just about the last place worth going," the logger says. The sun makes colors in his beard.

"Is she your girlfriend?" I say. "The one who gave you the suspenders?"

The logger looks down, first at one suspender, then the other. "She moved away," he says.

"Joey, this guy I know, his girlfriend moved away too," I say. "Deedee Lamont. She used to live up Wildcat Creek, but now she's in town studying toothcleaning at the community college. Joey moved to town for awhile, but he came back because college is a waste of time, and he'd rather work at the mill anyway. You can get your teeth done for fourteen dollars, but it takes forever, and Joey says her aim's not very good, so you swallow lots of blood."

The logger leans back on his hands and stretches out his legs. His steel toes almost touch mine. My toes are pink, pink, pink from how green the moss is.

"Deedee Lamont thinks Joey still lives with his parents," I say.

***

Off in the distance the river comes and goes with the wind. I eat jerky and swallow another Budweiser, not near as nasty as the first one. I make a net of my fingers to hold myself up by my knees. The logger asks if I want to share the last beer with him.

"You can have it," I say. Things are tilty enough already.

"And whatever else you want," I say, meaning what's left of the chocolate chip cookies and salmon jerky, but mostly meaning something else.

He watches me with eyes like a deer when it's not hunting season, when you can watch each other for as long as it takes the sun to rearrange all the light in the forest. Until the deer twitches one ear and goes back to chewing whatever it was chewing before it saw you.

I unweave my fingers and lean back on my hands. The sun shines down on my face, while the logger takes the last beer and empties it down his throat.

***

One thing about Joey is I knew him first. Before we did anything. There was the time Mama paid him to come over and fix the car, and then later, when she couldn't drive any more, Mama employed Joey to bring what we needed from town. By the time Joey started looking at me a certain way,

I'd already had some practice pressing my lips against the bathroom mirror.

The logger is looking at me that way.

The moss is wet and cool and deep. My fingers can't even touch bottom, it's that deep.

"Have you ever been with a man?" the logger says.

"Joey's almost twenty," I say.

"I guess not then," he says. And the logger touches me as light as you can touch something and still call it touching. It's how you touch a lady slipper when you tip its head up. That's how his hands are on my face. But mostly it's his eyes. Not closed, like Joey pretending I'm Deedee Lamont, the logger keeps his eyes open and nice all over me. My arms give out, and I fall back on his gray wool jacket with my head in the moss. The sun makes a halo in his frizzy hair. His mouth is coming closer and closer and he's about to kiss me, I just know it. But then something happens, and his mouth is nowhere near mine. I look over at what made him jerk his head up. It's a squirrel, a squirrel who's running crazy circles around and around and around on one of the fresh stumps, too crazy confused to make a sound. Anyone would laugh at how that squirrel's acting, if you didn't know how it must feel.

The logger doesn't laugh. We both sit up, and he takes my hand and holds it in both of his, like we're at a funeral together. The squirrel keeps on and on and on running hopeless circles. The logger finally interrupts it. "You better go find yourself someplace else to live," he says.

The squirrel stops dead and seems to notice us for the first time. It stands crouched on four legs, its tail up in the air. Then it's gone, just like that.

I lay back down and try to get back to how it was before.

The logger takes one more look around, then he smiles down on me. But now I've got tears crawling out my eyes, they puddle cold inside my ear. The logger asks me if I'm okay and that does it, now it's coming out my nose too.

The logger gets up and walks away. I sit up and have to bite my arm to keep from making noises, but then he's back with a water bottle.

"This is as good a time as any for me to go on up to Alaska," he says.

It could be the Sahara Desert, that's how hard I drink. Then I press my forehead into my arms on my knees and rock back and forth on the soft ground.

"Yeah, I know," the logger says. "I shouldn't have tried to kiss you."

You don't know, is what I'm thinking. You don't know anything. I try to think about Alaska instead. What kind of trees they have up there, maybe no trees, maybe nothing but snow.

Bones poking up from the snow, if you die there.

***

The sun moves. We're covered in shade. Quiet as two stumps, sitting there side by side, close but not touching. So close I can smell his own living smell underneath the gas and chainsaw smells.

"Well," the logger says.

The clouds close in on what's left of the sun. I know I'm supposed to get off my butt and give him his jacket, but I can't. I can't let him leave. Not yet.

"This is kind of off the subject," I say, "but I was wondering if you might know. Do coyotes eat things that are already dead, or do they have to kill it theirselves?"

The logger scratches his beard. "I can't say for certain,"

he says, "but I guess a coyote would eat just about anything. Why?"

"Just wondering," I say. "There's this coyote nosing around Mama's trailer after dark. Joey saw its green eyes."

Shimmery brown, the logger's eyes. They don't jitter away like Joey's, always making you think he's got somewhere else he's supposed to be. So I go on. "The other night Joey went out to shoot the coyote," I say, "but he got into mud over the tops of his sneakers and had to come back in to yell at me. He said anybody with half a pint of brain knows you're not supposed to dig up your garden this early, you're supposed to wait till the dirt's had a chance to dry out."

The logger doesn't know what I'm talking about.

"Joey thinks Mama got taken to her sister's," I say. My voice is so reckless it sets off a crow. "And the reason he found me living all by myself in Mama's trailer is because they don't have any room for me at my aunt's house."

The crow keeps on hollering from on high.

"Joey asked wasn't I scared living alone all by myself," I say. "He said if I wanted he could come keep me company once in awhile."

The crow is flying circles in the empty hole in the sky where there used to be a tree.

"My mama never had any sisters," I say. "Or brothers. Or anyone, just me. She said I'd have to live in a foster home after she's gone."

The logger takes me inside his arms. I press my face into the warm smell of his neck. I pull my face out and tell the rest. "I didn't have a coffin to put her in or anything, but Mama doesn't mind that, I know she doesn't. She said she'd rather enrich the soil than just lay around, one big hurt, making a nuisance of herself. I told her she wasn't a nuisance. I told her I wasn't learning anything in school anyway, but Mama said if I really wanted to help her I'd stop trying to make her eat. She made me promise not to call nine-one-one when things got bad."

The logger's eyes say, go on.

"So I didn't," I yell. "I didn't call nine-one-one."

The logger's eyes say, tell it all.

"I reckon Mama'd rather get taken off by a coyote than an ambulance," I say, and it's just about all I can do not to look at the picture that's painting itself inside my head.

***

The first hummingbird of the season.

It makes a pass at the logger's red gas can. Next the orange motor on his chainsaw. It checks out his yellow hard hat on the stump. Then it sees the rainbow-colored suspenders and buzzes up behind the logger. But the logger never sees the hummingbird behind his back.

The logger only has eyes for me.

***

We drive to the river in his pickup. The rocks I really want are too heavy, even for us both working together. But we find some nice ones, bigger than what a coyote could push around with its paws. The rocks are heavier than they look. The logger says I'm strong for a girl.

"From splitting firewood and lifting Mama," I say. I push the puffy sleeves of Mama's peasant blouse up to my shoulders. I show him my muscles. And then it starts raining, but we're too busy to be bothered. We put the rocks in an artful pile over the mud behind the trailer, then go into the forest and dig up some maidenhair ferns and bleeding hearts and whatever else looks pretty that isn't rooted too deep. It's landscape art, nicer even than a marker. The evening sun opens under the clouds and throws diamonds all over the ferns and bleeding hearts.

"Damn fine rock garden," the logger says. His rainbow-colored suspenders are ten times brighter than any real rainbow. And now a bunch of new pictures are painting themselves inside my head. I figure I'll just ask him. As soon as we're done saying a few words over Mama, I'll ask. I'll ask the logger if he'll let me come with him up to Alaska. He already knows I'm strong for a girl, and if that's not enough I can always make myself full of temptations. And once I'm there, once I'm up in Alaska, if he gets tired of me like Joey, there's always the possibility of wolves.

At the Intersection of Heaven and Hell

A skinny girl wearing nothing but boots and goggles pumps toward me on her bike. I get a quick look at her nipples before she's lost in the dust. People drift in and out of sight, we're all wandering around dusted with white playa powder. Young and old alike, our hair, our beards, our moustaches are all the same grey.

All these dust storms keep blowing me back to Iraq. Not that I've ever been to Iraq, but this is what I do these days, I try to imagine what it's like in that other doomed-to-hell place. It's been five months since the invasion. Five months and the devil knows how much longer until it's over. If ever. My buddy Wayne said coming to Burning Man would take my mind off Iraq. If nothing else, at least the naked chicks were supposed to give me something fresh to obsess over.

Yeah, right.

So we drove Wayne's truck across the mountains and through endless miles of sagebrush, through the night and half the next day to get to this ephemeral mayhem in the middle of this flat white desert. We entered Black Rock City, threw up a couple of tents and a canopy, and then Wayne changed into a silky red slip – not my thing, but hey, it's a free country – and he took off on his bike to view the art. And now it looks like the air has cleared enough that I can lift my goggles and try to enjoy the view of the two girls walking in front of me. Their thonged asses, how they work their walk into the beat, the techno beat that's machine-gunning from on high from some metal tower. These girls look about the same age as my daughter, my Melissa. The short one's got an eagle tattooed across her back. Devil knows, she's stuck with it for the rest of her life.

And I'm just a dick-in-the-dirt tourist in search of a can.

The air clears to a painful brilliance, and I can see where a distant row of porta-pots stand side by side like soldiers in the sun. Bleak mountains off in the distance, not a breath of living green, and that missing piece of horizon where a dust devil is gathering itself to blast us into the next whiteout.

I get in line behind a deeply tanned guy with a sweaty beer bottle. He's talking to a nipple-pierced girl who's cultivating a killer sunburn. He's telling her about some camp run by fishermen from Oregon, bragging how he gorged on plate after plate of free salmon and tuna. I see the guy shoveling blackened fish into his greasy mouth. I see the girl getting fried by the sun. I see her blister and peel and in twenty or so years sprout a malignant melanoma which will metastasize to her brain and kill her dead. And if she has a child by then, that poor child will have to be raised by the random scruff who seeded it.

Porta-pot doors squeak open and slam shut. Some woman with the voice of a heavy smoker announces to the crowd that she just had the best shit ever. People cheer.

Not my thing, but hey.

I untie the orange bandana from around my neck. It's for slipping over my mouth when the dust gets bad, but I shake it out and lay it across the burnt girl's shoulders. Before she can say anything, I turn and ask the fish guy for directions to the free fish.

He shakes his head and laughs. "It doesn't matter," he says. "With greedheads like me around, they've gotta be out of fish by now." He heads into the next empty can. Another one opens up and the girl tries to give me back my bandana.

"No, please," I say, as if it weren't already too late. "It's yours," as if anything I do could make a difference.

***

Wayne and I are drinking gin and tonics. We're in lawnchairs under the scant shade of our canopy. Wayne is naked now, other than white socks and a pair of puppy slippers.

Three black jets spurt from the horizon. They arc over the playa as one evil thing. The noise is cruel. One, two, three, four raging passes, then they vanish across the mountain range to the east. If this were a movie, we'd have a mid-air collision, they'd burst into flames, smoking metal would fall from the sky.

"What do you think, man?" says Wayne. "Could we be a more tempting target? Thirty-thousand cultural creatives all in one place and no real buildings to get damaged?"

I squint toward the spot where the jets disappeared. After the jets the techno beat sounds mellow as rain.

"They'd blame it on terrorists," I say.

"Dick Cheney's wet dream," says Wayne.

***

I wake from an afternoon nap swaddled in sweat, doomed to hell by some freaky nightmare and a jackhammering noise that shouldn't be this close to my tent. I try to get out, but the zipper's jammed. I'm in an oven, I'm on my knees, I'm in the direct path of this noise. For all I know, I'm about to be the next sucker to get creamed under the truck tires of some drunk. And still, the demented zipper won't work! I find the knife in my pocket and slash through the door. I tumble out and spring to my feet. Stand free over my wrecked tent. The dry desert air feels cool for a moment as it flows over my wet skin.

Wayne is giving me a hard time from his lawnchair. "Was that necessary?" he says.

Okay. So they've got their generator going full blast at the next camp over. I fold the blade and put my knife back in my jeans. I go sit by Wayne in the shade. Some half-dressed prom queen who calls him or herself Nola is behind Wayne giving him a backrub.

"I was deep into this Clockwork Orangey dream," I say. "I was at a window and a bunch of punks come roaring up our driveway on motorcycles. They're all black leather and chains."

"Ooh la la," says Nola. Nola has large pink gums and teeth like a horse.

I continue. "Meanwhile, Melissa comes up from the basement."

"You guys have a basement?" says Wayne. His eyes are closed and his head lolls back into Nola's belly.

"This is a goddamn *dream,*" I say. "So Melissa goes out there and I do nothing to stop her. I stand there looking out the window while these maggots get off their bikes and start punching and kicking my daughter to the ground."

"So what'd you do?" says Wayne.

"That's the point," I whine. "I did *nothing*!"

I get up and walk over to the cooler by Wayne's van. I take out a wet bottle, suck down half a beer, return to my lawnchair. "And then I woke up broiling in my tent with a goddamn stuck zipper," I say.

Wayne opens his eyes. "The trick to zippers in this dust," says Wayne, "is to rub them with soap."

"Don't get me started on the dust," says Nola, still kneading Wayne's back. "I brought my saxophone out here once? It cost me nine-hundred dollars to get it cleaned." Nola makes mournful eyes under fake eyelashes.

"They're saying on the news that dust is the reason why things aren't working in Iraq," I say.

"I thought it was sand," says Wayne.

"I thought it was American Imperialism," says Nola.

The sun roasts across my back. I edge my lawnchair into the shrinking patch of shade, to where my knees are almost touching Wayne's. I lean forward with both my hands wrapped hard around the beer bottle.

"Tell me your honest opinion," I say. "You know how Melissa is. If a tank were headed for her tent, do you think she'd slash her way out?"

Wayne gives me a look.

"If her zipper were stuck!" I yell.

"Man, you are seriously tweaking," says Wayne.

"I mean this is a girl who washes and recycles those plastic bags you put your lettuce in. This is a girl who does *mending*." I drop my empty beer bottle to the ground and slap my hand against the right knee of my pants. "Check it out," I say.

Wayne leans over. His shoulders slip free of Nola's hands, which immediately go to adjusting his or her platinum wig and rhinestone tiara. Wayne examines the tidy little stitches along the edge of my knee patch.

"See what I mean?" I say. "Don't you think a girl like Melissa would *hesitate* before slashing her way out of a tent?"

Wayne leaves his hand on my knee. "Steve," he says.

"What?" I say.

"Listen to me, bro." Wayne tightens his hold on my knee. "Your kid in Iraq?" he says. "That's not your fault."

***

And then later that night I see Melissa, her long hair flamboyant in the wind. She's seated on a chariot that's spurting blue-green fire from a couple of flame-throwers. I run after her until the chariot is lost in the overall chaos and illumination.

Wait a minute, wasn't there a phone call? A phone call where Melissa told me she had cut her hair.

No way could her hair grow back so soon.

And now I see that I've done it again, lost my bearings in the neon roar of Black Rock City at night, lost Wayne and Nola and the entire band of pilgrims I started the evening with.

Yes, this is something I now remember. Melissa left her amazing hennaed hair at some training camp in Texas.

I pull up the sarong at my waist, it keeps trying to fall off, this flimsy piece of cloth that Nola talked me into when it was too hot for anything else. But now the world is coming unraveled in this wind, and I'm cold and clueless as to how to get back to camp. All I can do is wander from fire to fire and search for something familiar in the shadowy faces of strangers.

Until, between fires, I get hit by a dust devil. It funnels me into the mouth of a windsock tube, I push through a curtain of blowing fabric into the pulsing soundtrack of a large tent, and now I'm in the smoky red haze of some kind of club that smells of incense and burnt hair. I rub grit from my eyes and behold half-naked people in shackles on the ground. A girl in handcuffs, a guy in chains, someone else holding something that might be a cattle prod.

"Master or slave?" says a man's voice near my ear. A woman covered in tattoos approaches me smiling.

"Not my thing," I say. I tighten the knot on my sarong and back out the door. "But hey," I say, "I can feel the love."

And it's true, even in there.

***

A bunch of early risers, or those of us who never went to bed, are waiting in line for bags of ice. Even at this hour, the playa still pulses to the beat, some techno trance DJ working the morning. Next to me in line is a woman holding a parasol. She's got the well-rested look of a morning person. And here is a guy wandering around spray-painted purple. His cock dangles loose between his legs. This guy's cock is so big it makes me want to get a tape measure. I'd hate to see it hard. Meanwhile all of us ordinary citizens get to imagine what he does with it at night. We get to stare at this purple thing from behind our mirror sunglasses.

Except for the woman with the parasol, she slides her sunglasses down to the tip of her nose and gives herself an eyefull. Her long gauzy dress, her pale protected skin, the shape of her nose in profile, if this were a movie she'd be Meryl Streep.

The woman notices me noticing her in the ice line and both of us noticing the purple cock.

We're having a moment.

And now she winks at me, pushes the sunglasses back up

her nose, and lifts her parasol so its shade covers us both. We move forward with the ice line as if we were a couple. I offer to take a turn holding the parasol. Behind us, the subject is Burning Man art.

"Dude, what's with all the *religious* bullshit?"

"Yeah, one more temple and I'm gonna puke."

"It's not about religion," says a girl's voice. "It's spiritual."

"Same thing."

"No it's not."

"Well, whatever, it's not art."

"Oh, these kids," whispers the woman, as if we shared such insights all the time. She turns to look at them, and I shift the shade of the parasol so it covers her face.

"Ya'll want to know art?" says the woman. Her voice is spiced by some kind of Deep South.

"Sure," says a girl with dirt-colored dreads. They've all got metal doodads hung from various body parts.

The woman lifts her sunglasses to the top of her head and squints into the naked light. She's older this way, the creases around her eyes, but I'd follow her as far as she'd let me across this hopeless desert. Just holding her parasol, and I'm cured of being a tourist.

"Nine 'leven," says the woman in her adorable accent. "Now *tha-yut* was a work of art."

The air throbs. Serpentine sounds spiral around the subwoofer heartbeat. No one says a word. And I'm not sure what undoes me more, the woman's words or the eerie sense that we all know exactly what she's saying.

***

High noon on Wayne's bike and I'm rolling a straight line toward the temple. The temple floats on waves of heat in the distance, its watery onion-shaped minarets spiking the sky. Between me and the temple a lone man stands in his shadow on the empty playa. He won't give an inch as I approach, so I swerve around him at the last moment and see that he's pissing. He could be playa art, an installation titled, "Man Who Thinks He Can Piss a Hole to China."

As if I haven't drilled a few holes into the playa myself.

The temple turns out to be a good place to escape the sun. I hang out under its shade and read the graffiti. The graffiti on the walls is a bunch of prayers and poems and apologies, all about dead people. Photographs are taped up and down the columns and walls. A studio portrait of an old couple. A guy on a snowboard suspended in a deep blue sky. And here's a middle-aged woman with pigtails and a backwards baseball cap. Someone's mom, too cute to be dead.

One useful thing I could write about Melissa's mom is that she might have been more careful about avoiding the sun, or at least used sunscreen.

If Melissa were here she'd want to put up a picture. Melissa has all the pictures I never took of her mom. Linda and I tanked too early for pictures, too early to have anything between us but the baby in her belly. And when Linda got on a plane to Hawaii, six months pregnant, that was the end of that. Linda kept Melissa to herself for twelve years and then she died and I got Melissa and Melissa got nothing but a bunch of pictures of Linda posing on various beaches. Whichever photos Melissa didn't take to Iraq must be in boxes with the rest of the stuff she packed away before deployment.

Deployment. Now there's a word.

I tried to stop her. I found my daughter turning her

room upside down, a clutter of boxes, books, and clothes. She was sitting on the floor surrounded by a platoon of stuffed animals. "You don't need to do this," I said from the doorway.

"Yes I do," said Melissa. "I want you to make this room back into a studio, how it was before I came to live with you. You should get back into clay. Get back into your art."

"Fuck art," I said. "If I hadn't wasted my time with art, I might have earned us some money to put you through college."

Melissa made a nest of white tissue paper in a cardboard box. She put in her beanie babies and taped shut the box.

"You're not going to do this," I said. I went in and sat on the bed. "Now that you're all packed," I said, "we can move to Canada."

"Dad," she said. Melissa never called me dad, up until then I'd only been Steve to her. This new word scared me. She must have seen it in my face, because she reached out her hand and touched my foot.

"Dad," she said, "this isn't the sixties."

The things I could write on these walls about Melissa, if I were the type. If I thought it could make a difference.

And now I notice the fat magic marker abandoned on a bench. I go pick it up. Pop the cap and have a sniff. The sudden hit of fumes comes as a surprise, I expected it to have gone dry.

Forget it, this so-called Temple of Honor with its filigreed remembrances has nothing to do with me or my hellbent daughter. And my Melissa is not dead. My Melissa is alive, either in or outside of Baghdad.

Jesus Christ, Baghdad.

And now I see the man who seduced my daughter.

His stiff back, his clean-shaved face, his stuffed jacket with its insignia and brass. He called it an open door to higher education. He called it a chance to see the world. He called it a peacetime army.

I bite the plastic cap between my teeth. Hold the black magic marker like a knife ready to stab someone in the heart. I write these slanted words on the temple wall: STAFF SERGEANT CLIFF HOSKINS, US ARMY 6th RECRUITING BRIGADE, YOU LOUSY LYING HEADHUNTER. MAY IT BE YOUR CHILD IN PLACE OF MINE.

***

What was I thinking?

I headed off into the darkness after sampling at a bunch of free bars, and now I'm flat in the moonless middle of nowhere. I try to cover myself with what's left of Nola's sarong after I cut it loose from the bike chain. I hold a tassel to my heart and roll myself up like a burrito. I turn my face toward the lights of Black Rock City juking on the horizon, and I look north of the city to where the Man stands alone, a blue neon colossus on top of a pyramid. And up here we have Mars overhead, pulsing in a trance dance of its very own.

Does Melissa know it's been sixty or so thousand years since Mars has come this close?

And does the Iraqi desert have such winds? Does the Iraqi night get so cold?

Coming toward me are a distant pair of headlights, closer and closer until I'm nailed in the blinding beam.

"Sorry, dude," says a voice, and the lights go out. I drop my hands from my face. It turns out to be just a couple of rangers on patrol in a jeep. They get out with their flashlights, and now I have to convey to these kids in

Utilikilts that I'm not another E-tard they need to scrape from the playa and deliver to medical camp. They give the standard lecture about dehydration and leave me a tall bottle of water, along with a nice fleece blanket.

I fall asleep, weepy with love for these young heroes.

And wake up tilting toward the blue light of morning. I may be cheek-to-cheek with the playa, but I'm still losing my balance. The beat of some all night rave comes and goes, as elastic as the wind. Black Rock City growls with the rumble of a few thousand generators.

Things have been going on in this way for about a week now. Just one simple moment of silence, is that asking too much?

I manage to get up on one elbow and suckle water from the bottle, then fall to my back while the sky gets an infusion of sunrise. This is going to be one hell of a morning after. I'm shivering with cold and my body feels like someone rolled over it with a tank. I remember something I overheard about a hot spring pool in an oasis of green, hidden somewhere on the edge of this desert. That is absolutely the place to be right now.

I drag my sorry ass off the ground and huddle into my blanket of fleece, stumble barefoot across the playa. Stretched out before my toes is a long skinny Arab in a burka.

At least my shadow knows where we're going.

But those distant mountains don't get any closer. My shadow shrivels into this desiccated little blob under my feet. I abandon my blanket to the heat. The wind steals the sarong. And now comes vomiting, diarrhea, thirst. My water's gone.

The devil knows this wouldn't be the first time some

idiot wandered off naked and alone to die in the desert. But who am I fooling? I know I'm faking it. I know I won't die out here, I know I'll be rescued by the next patrol of Black Rock Rangers. Yet here I am staging some cliché movie where I get to stand at the intersection of Heaven and Hell and make my deal with God.

I fall to my knees in my ridiculous little shadow, I play out my part. Okay, God, here's the deal: Deploy *me* to the wasteland. You know what I'm saying here.

***

Early evening and Mary Magdalena has pulled her mobile footwash cart into our camp. I'm wrecked in my lawnchair, fresh from mainlining saltwater at medical. Three hours of soothing IV. And now my filthy cracked feet are in the hands of this sweet-breasted girl. Like everything else around here, Mary's hands guide me into some strange melding of pleasure and pain. Meanwhile Wayne, Nola, and a bunch of Germans with names too weird to remember are all getting glitzed and glittered for the big burn. Between costume changes, they're all toking this and snorting that.

At least they don't try to suck me into their scene. Other than Nola batting his or her eyelashes my way. Nola, who found and delivered Mary Magdalena. I give Nola a thumbs up, and even though it's not my thing, I blow Nola a kiss.

But back to Mary Magdalena. She kneels before me on a small mud-caked carpet. Her shape is elfin, I can see it all through her transparent green gown. Narrow hips like a boy, girlish breasts that may or may not be done growing, pubes shaved into a Mohawk. She pours cool water from a plastic jug over my feet, which sets off a whole new wave of whatever it is, pleasure, pain. The water runs muddy into a green Rubbermaid. She works over my feet with a wet washcloth, dries them with a frayed towel. Now she rubs in scented oil, pulls her fingers between my toes. Her fingernails are tipped with black crescents of dirt and this is where I lose it, this is where I tilt from giddy to something else. I close my eyes tight, but it's too late, I'm already pierced by those beautiful black crescents of dirt tracing the fingernails of Mary Magdalena. I close my throat, but something squeaks out.

"It's okay," says Mary. She gives my foot a comforting squeeze.

But no, it's not okay. It is not okay to turn into the statue of a father when my child tells me she's in the army and then go all blubbery at the sight of some little mama's dirty fingernails. It is not okay to lose myself in the kindness of strangers while the devil knows what cruelties await my daughter. It is not okay to feel the love in the middle of some hedonistic party while the one person who matters falls into the fires of hell.

"It's okay," says Mary Magdalena. She holds my foot quite still in her hand. She looks up from where she's kneeling, her eyes completely open to mine, and I see that she's holding me and my foot hostage. I see that she will not let go until I do. I see what she's up to, how she's waiting for me to surrender to the magical power of reflexology or whatever it is she wants to believe in.

Oh, these kids.

And this is the last thought before I give way to what she wants. Oh these kids, and now I'm crying and now I'm gone and now this crying is something that is happening without me.

After the crying comes a calm where Mary Magdalena and I are nothing but eyes watching each other. Then I remember myself, I knuckle my eyes. "They dosed me with two bags of saltwater," I say. "It looks like they went over the fill line."

Mary goes back to work. She puts down my foot and pulls a tube of chapstick from a beaded bag at her waist. She holds the foot back up and says, "This one needs a little something extra, it's cracked deep." She rubs chapstick into the ravine on my heel.

And I title this piece, "Girl Who Attends to Man's Cracked Sole."

***

Nola has used his or her pull to get us on the crowded upper deck of *La Contessa*. This is a tall Spanish galleon now rolling to a stop behind a ring of thirty-thousand people. Everyone down on the playa is going crazy. They're wearing glow sticks and blinky things that bob up and down with the drumbeat.

"They've got enough naked fire dancers down there to populate their own planet," someone says.

"Enough drum power to wake up the snakes in Washington," says someone else.

From up here on *La Contessa,* the night is spread out like a sacrificial offering. And here's the centerpiece, the Man, this blue neon deity who stands on top of a pretentious pyramid and towers over the whole scene.

"You wanna know how all this started?" says a guy who's pressed against the wooden rail next to me. I don't know if he's talking to me or to someone else, there's such a crush of bodies up here in the dark. But his voice goes on, one voice among the many. "Some dude's girlfriend ditched him for another guy, I think it was his best friend. So the dude has a party. He builds a wooden statue of the guy who stole his chick, and he burns this statue on the beach, and everyone digs it, so the dude does it again every summer until there's so many folks coming they get kicked off the beach."

Something is changing about the Man. He's lifting his arm, he's growing a bright red heart.

"Born out of pain," says the guy, "the untold history of Burning Man."

"Well, you just told it, honey," says Nola's voice, from my other side on the rail.

The Man now has a red cartoon heart that's throbbing in time. This is something new, this brilliant red heart in the center of the Man's blue neon ribs. And now we have rockets and fireworks and explosions. The pyramid ignites into flames, the crowd screams its head off as the Man is shot through with fire, even as his heart is keeping the beat. And everyone's shouting like *they* did this, myself included. We're all pyromaniacs at heart.

And then later, after the Man has fallen, after the party has moved back into Black Rock City, Nola and Wayne walk, one on each side of me, as I limp back to camp. We skirt around the acres of burning rubble, and I say, "Just think about Baghdad."

Wayne sighs. He doesn't want to think about Baghdad. He doesn't want me to think about Baghdad. Wayne brought me here to take my mind off Baghdad.

"Flames, cacophony, and chaos," says Nola.

It's all I can do not to go weepy again, that Nola is willing to think about Baghdad.

"The difference is," Nola goes on, "the difference is that *these* people have no interest in killing each other."

And we walk on across the dark playa, no longer sure of our direction, because with the Man burned down, there's nothing but Mars to use for navigation.

Dalai Lama

Daisy first called to tell me about the Dalai Lama in early May. Les was out of it in the bedroom and I was wrapped up in an old quilt on the sofa watching *All My Children*. I hit the mute button on the TV remote and wished I had a remote for the answering machine.

"We did it, Robin! We got the Dalai Lama to come to Alaska. Pick up the damn phone. I know you're there, Robin. I know you never go anywhere before noon."

On the silent television, it was the Providence Breakthrough commercial where some woman is mushing her sled dogs across the entire beauty of winter.

"The Dalai *Lama*, Robin. In *Anchorage*. Sunday, the fifteenth. You've gotta come, I'll be super pissed if you don't. Not that you'd care about that, but you should come anyway."

The woman finally got herself through rehab, which is supposedly why she and her dogs are having such a fucking great time.

"Robin?"

Then Daisy yelled my name like when we were kids,

right before she was about to punch me. "Rob *IN*!"

I switched to the black and white movie channel. *African Queen*. Katherine Hepburn looked about as hyper as Daisy sounded.

"You better call me," Daisy said. "Good *bye*!"

Daisy left messages on my machine every day for a week. The last time she called about the Dalai Lama was during *The Young and The Restless*. Les was next to me on the sofa, picking at his back. Almost two years after he got hit and Les was still squeezing pieces of the other guy's windshield from his skin.

"I'll come pick you up," Daisy's voice said.

I got up from the sofa. My foot knocked over a can of beer.

"You can bring Les," Daisy was saying. "Les or whoever you're living with these days. How would I know, since you never tell me anything."

I hit the delete button. The flashing red light went dark.

"Bring me where?" Les said.

I stared at the empty answering machine. "Why do you have to always put your beer on the floor?" I said.

"Why do you have to always kick it over?" Les said.

I found the towel we use to wipe mud off Growler. It was over something sticky on the kitchen floor. Using my toes, I shuffled the towel to the braided rug, kicked aside the beer can, and stepped up and down on the towel until the bottom of one sock was wet. I got back into the sofa. Now it was *Guiding Light*.

"Bring me where?" Les said.

"To see the Dalai Lama," I said.

"What's that?" Les said.

"Nothing," I said. "Nothing you'd be interested in."

We went to bed after *Saturday Night Live* and then someone was banging on the cabin door. Daylight was seeping in along the edge of the black curtain, but that didn't mean anything. This part of May it could still be the middle of the night. I remembered the crank in the Krusteaz box, pot in my daypack, crosstops—no, we'd run out of crosstops. Then I heard who it was.

"Rob *IN*!" That voice.

Growler was out there barking his fool head off from the end of his chain. I tried to stand up, but started to lose it, so I bent over naked and lowered myself to all fours. I felt around and found my poncho on the floor. Then sat back on my heels and pushed my head through the hole, which made my hair shoot sparks that crackled like insects. I climbed up and sat on the edge of the bed and waited for the silver insulation on the wall to stop moving.

Les had his head under a black pillow. His arms were tucked beneath his body. I must have pulled the blankets off him when I got up. He looked like a broken marble statue against the black sheet. No head. No arms. Nice firm ass, how I wished mine looked. Long back, narrow and smooth, except for the scars.

"Rob *IN*!" Daisy's voice so you'd think the house was on fire. Daisy's hand busy as a woodpecker at the door.

I pulled the blankets over Les. Tucked them around his neck. His breath from under the pillow was warm on my fingers.

Growler was still barking, probably about to strangle himself on the chain. The chain was Growler's consequence for hiding under the bed and chewing the crotches out of all my panties. That was after I yelled at him for eating the salad bowl, which happened to be the only nice thing in the kitchen, the only thing not plastic or aluminum.

I went to the door and opened it. The May light hurt my eyes.

"Growler!" I yelled. "Shut up! Stop it, Growler! Down!"

Growler lowered his chin to the ground, but kept his rear end up. You could hear his tail whacking the chain. You'd think it would hurt.

Daisy.

Daisy stood there on our porch, dressed like she thought she was a spring fairy. All blue and green and lavender. The multi-layered look, skirts, scarves, shawl. Surrounding Daisy, all that in-your-face May light.

"I could never keep a dog chained up like that," Daisy said.

Why bother to tell Daisy we were only dogsitting Growler until Les' brother got out of jail. I put up my arm and tried to shield my eyes from spring.

Daisy reached one hand through the doorway. She took hold of my hair, and right away I grabbed a handful of hers, soft and wavy, a lighter and cleaner blonde than mine. If she started pulling, I'd pull hers back just as hard. Like when we were kids, and our mom had to pry our fingers loose once we started screaming, neither one of us ever the first to let go.

"Oh my God, Robin," Daisy said. "When did you start dreading you hair?"

"I don't know, whenever," I said.

"Has mom seen it?" Daisy said.

I shook my head no. Then we both spoke together in the Mom voice, "*White* people should *never* wear dreadlocks."

Daisy pulled open the side of my poncho and looked at my naked body. "Get dressed," she said. "We can't be late."

"I'm not going," I said.

"Bullshit!" Daisy said.

I stood in the doorway.

"You've got to," Daisy said. "It's the Dalai Lama."

"Get over it, Daisy," I said. "Just get over trying to save me."

"Come on," Daisy said. "Please?"

"I'm not you, Daisy. You don't even know me!" I said.

Off in the woods behind the cabin you could hear a robin. *Cheerily cheer-up cheerio*. When had they come back?

"Please?" Daisy said.

"No."

Cheerily cheer-up cheerio. The air had that smell of things starting to turn green.

"But I want you to, Robin!" Daisy shouted. So loud she got Growler barking again.

"Take it somewhere else, Daisy," I said. "Why can't you just leave me and my crappy life alone?"

"Fine!" Daisy said. Her footsteps were too loud across the porch. What was she wearing on her feet?

Daisy headed for her car. She held her layers of blue and green and lavender up from the mud, her fists tight on her skirts. She turned her head and yelled over her shoulder, "Fuck you, Robin! Fuck *you* and your whole fucking white trash, fucking loser, fucking shitty life!" Daisy wasn't looking where she was going.

Cheerily cheer-up cheerio.

"Daisy, look out!" I yelled. But it was too late.

Purple cowboy boots. One of them splat in Growler's turdpile. Daisy lifted her foot and looked at it over her shoulder.

Daisy screaming, Growler barking, and the birds all

cheerily cheer-up cheerio-ing.

Les came out on the porch in his sand-colored Carhartts, no shirt, one pink nipple showing. He smoked a cigarette with one hand and picked glass from his back with the other.

"Cool boots," Les said. He held a piece of the other guy's windshield up to his eye, then flicked it off the porch. The May air snuck in through the open sides of my poncho. I pulled the poncho closed and hugged it around my waist.

"My boots," Daisy wailed. She sounded so bummed, I wanted to do something.

I got one of the rusted folding chairs from the card table in the kitchen and took it out to the porch. Daisy scraped her boot on the edge of a porch step, then sat and held onto the seat of the chair with her leg stuck straight out while I knelt in front of her and tried to wiggle off the purple cowboy boot. Her calf was warm and smooth on my knuckles. Daisy was shaving her legs again and that meant she was fucking someone. Gorgeous guy, meaningful life, I didn't ask. I gave the boot a yank. Daisy's purple cowboy boot came free and kicked me in the chest.

Wet dogshit on my poncho.

"Oh Robin," Daisy said. "That's your poncho from our trip to Mexico. Bummer."

"Don't worry about it," I said.

I took Daisy's purple cowboy boot inside and dropped it in the toilet to soak, then pulled the poncho off over my head, making sure not to get dogshit in my face or hair. When I came out of the bathroom, the TV was on, no sound. Les was rolling a joint at the card table and Daisy was sitting there in one purple cowboy boot and one purple sock. Daisy sat on the edge of the sofa the way you'd sit on a wet log if you didn't want to get your butt dirty. I smelled the cabin through Daisy's nose. Stale cigarette smoke, spilt beer, mold, and rot. And now dogshit.

I walked by naked and threw the poncho out on the porch. Then put on one of Les' workshirts from the nail by the door. My fingers felt around back to be sure it covered my bare butt, then went and sat on the edge of the sofa next to Daisy. Les came and sat at the other end. He ran his tongue along the joint, then lit and puffed it to life. Les coughed and passed the joint to Daisy. Daisy said no thanks, but Les was turned the other way, coughing and snorting smoke, still holding the bouncing joint in front of Daisy's face. She finally took the joint between her thumb and forefinger and tried to pass it to me.

"It's just weed," I said. I kept my hands in my lap.

Daisy held the joint in front of her eyes and turned it back and forth. "I haven't done this since high school," she said.

"Go on," I said. "It won't kill you."

Daisy put the tip between her puckered lips. Her lipstick was the color of fireweed, just like her nail polish. She looked into my eyes like she was proving something, then sucked hard on the loosely rolled joint. It was about to fall apart. Daisy took the joint out of her mouth and used her tongue to wet the place where a crack was burning up the side of the joint. Then, still holding her breath, Daisy smiled at me like she'd won an argument and passed me the repaired joint. I took it this time. Daisy let out her breath and sank back into the sofa between me and Les.

Les' face was long and twisted, trying to see his back. There was a spot on his shoulder where he'd squeezed out blood.

Daisy scootched down to my end of the couch.

Me and Daisy and Les passed the joint between us. Daisy forgot what happens when you're in the middle. She started taking a hit every time it went by. We were all sunk low in the busted springs of the sofa. Me and Daisy squished into each other and Les at the other end, channel surfing with no sound.

The TV flashed a slow strobe of pictures, in time with someone's heart beating. Daisy's body was warm against my side. I covered the white of my thighs with some extra skirt from Daisy's overflow of blue and green and lavender.

"What time is it?" Daisy suddenly yelled. She made a fist and punched a hard knuckle into my arm, then rose from the sofa like a fish breaking water. "Hurry up, Robin!" she said. "Go get dressed or we'll miss the Dalai Lama."

I went to the bedroom, used my foot to sort through the pile of clothes and crotchless panties on the floor. I heard Daisy ask Les, "Do you know what Robin did with my boot?" I kicked shut the bedroom door, put on my baggy corduroys, no underwear.

"Rob *IN*!" Daisy's voice was shrieking at me from the bathroom.

And then by Eagle River she was all over me about smoking in her car.

"Fine," I said. I reached across her face and threw the cigarette out the window she was opening. "You are some bitch sister, you know that, Daisy?" I said.

"Me?" Daisy shut the window on the trailing end of a scarf, then cracked it open and pulled in a length of lavender. She flung it over her shoulder and gave me this look like it was all my fault her stuff wanted to blow away. She said, "How would *you* feel if I stuck *your* boots in the toilet and never returned your phone calls?"

"It was just the bottom, and it was covered with dogshit, and all you ever want to do is brag about how great your life is compared to mine," I said.

"Whatever," Daisy said.

"Whatever," I said.

I tried to keep my eyes on the hard white edge of the Chugach Mountains, but all along the highway tree skeletons that had been dead for as long as I could remember were bleeding pale green into the sunlight. It was the kind of green that blames you for losing another entire winter.

I cried almost all the way to Anchorage, then I lay down and fell asleep with my head on Daisy's blue and green and lavender lap. Daisy's thigh was warm through the layers. Daisy's fingers were in my hair, playing with my dreads, while I slept.

Then Daisy's fingers were in my face, like when we were little and we'd squash and mold each other's faces. The car had stopped. Daisy was squeezing my mouth open with one hand and wagging my head back and forth.

"Wake up," she said. "Dammit, Robin, wake up. Look at all these people. We'll never see him. Hurry up!" Daisy worked me off her lap until I was upright in the passenger seat.

Too much sun came off the parked cars. Too much noise from the traffic in the street. I closed my eyes and heard the door open, then slam. I put my face down into the warm spot where Daisy had been. But then Daisy jerked me up by my arm from the passenger side. A cool draft came in through the open door.

"Rob *IN,*" Daisy said. "Come on!" She took my hand and pulled me out of the car into the hard light, where I almost fell over a body on the sidewalk. Some drunk native sleeping it off. I was tempted to join him down there, get back to my nap, but Daisy kept yanking my arm. She pulled me down Seventh Avenue, where a bunch of people were heading into the field next to the museum. Daisy was all Excuse me, Excuse me, Excuse me, stomping her purple cowboy boots through the middle of the crowd like she *belonged* in front of the ones we passed. Everyone was looking up over the heads of the people in front of them. One guy who smelled like a fishing boat was checking out Daisy. From her fireweed lips down to what he imagined was under her layers of blue and green and lavender. Then he saw me, and his eyes ping-ponged between our faces. He got that look that comes over certain guys when they get that we're identical twins, like he'd just found two blondes for the price of one.

"In your dreams," I said.

Daisy gave me one of her looks and yanked like she was trying to dismember my arm.

"What?" I said. "He doesn't care about the Dalai Lama. That loser's here for pussy."

"Just try to keep up, okay Robin?" Daisy said.

Daisy finally stopped when we got where we could see through the crowd to a bunch of monks in rust-colored robes. The monks had their heads shaved. Some of them were blowing into long skinny horns.

The noise of the horns, the smell of incense, people chanting like bees.

"Do you mind telling me what I'm doing here?" I said. "This is so *not* my scene."

"Shut up," Daisy said. "That's the Dalai Lama." She pointed to a guy draped in fall colors, sitting on some kind of throne up over the crowd.

"So?" I said.

The Dalai Lama stands up. He points his finger right into the part of the crowd where me and Daisy are standing. He comes down from his pulpit, and now he's in the crowd, and he's parting it like a line of coke. The people on both sides are falling to their knees, a couple of them flat out on their bellies. And this aisle opens up straight to the spot where me and Daisy are standing, and then the Dalai Lama's face is in my face, inches from my face, and he's got this bald head with glasses and this goofy look, like he's on ecstasy or something, and he whispers, "I see you."

I'm like, *huh*?

"Precious Jewel," he says. Like that's my name.

My first thought: you don't even *know* me.

My second thought: you think I'm Daisy.

And I reach out my hand to touch him on the shoulder, because I feel sorry for him, for how embarrassing it is for someone like him to blow it like this, with television cameras going and all these people watching. And I'm not saying anything out loud, but I'm looking into his eyes, and I'm thinking I should let him know it's okay, this happens all the time. Everyone gets me and Daisy mixed up. Even our parents. Like when we were little, all we ever needed to do was switch clothes and even our parents got confused.

Daisy's the one who came to see you, not me. Daisy's the one with the "Free Tibet" bumper sticker. Daisy, not me. I'm the one with the abortion. I'm the one who blew four years worth of college money in less than four months. I'm the one who flunked rehab. Daisy is the one you want. Daisy, not me. Daisy with her good grades and working her ass off to save the world.

All this was going through my head, not all separated

out like I'm telling it, but in one big flash. Meanwhile, he—the Dalai Lama—puts his hand on my shoulder, so we've each got one arm out resting on the other one's shoulder. His hand on Les' workshirt, my hand on his robe. How the shape of his shoulder fits just so in the palm of my hand, I don't want to do anything to mess it up. And now his face is coming closer to my face. Now he closes his eyes, and I can't blame him for not wanting to look, really, how I'm dressed. I haven't brushed my teeth or washed my face, no underwear. Still, he comes closer and he tips his head slightly down, and now he's touching his forehead into my forehead. His skin, my skin. Bones under skin.

The Dalai Lama's forehead pressed into my forehead, so all I could do was look down at the pavement.

Then he took a step back and that was it. The Dalai Lama turned and was gone. And the horns started up again and the buzz of the chanting. The people were blurry, but I could tell they were looking at me, and some of them had cameras and microphones, and I was like, what the fuck just happened?

Where was Daisy?

I looked around, and there was my sister, as clueless as me. All these people pushing past her. They were coming at me. A man with big smiling teeth had his hands out like he wanted to touch me. Some girl put an orange cloth over my head. Someone else was down on the ground with their hands on my hiking boots.

"Daisy?" I said. "Let's get outta here." I took the orange cloth off my head and gave it back to the girl. It covered her hands, praying at me. I slid my boot out from under someone's forehead. I grabbed my sister's hand and pulled it behind me through the crowd.

This time it wasn't just their backs, but all their eyes and faces. And hands—hands folded in prayer, hands palm-up to the sky, hands holding babies and children and each other. Everyone with the same smiley face under all that May light. And a woman's voice through a loudspeaker, saying words and words and words about His Holiness the Dalai Lama. His Holiness, His Holiness, His Holiness. Until finally we were alone and safe back in Daisy's parked car, with nothing but the slow sound of Sunday traffic moving by Daisy's window.

Outside my window, the native was in the exact same position as before. Still curled on his side, facing the other way on the sidewalk. I watched his back to see if he was breathing. He had the kind of hair I wanted. Straight blue-black hair you could pull a comb through.

"What did it feel like?" Daisy said. "When he touched you, what did that feel like?"

"Huh?" I said.

"The Dalai Lama?" Daisy said, all exasperated.

I just looked at Daisy, her eyes the same color of blue as mine.

"Rob *IN*!"

I looked away. The native was in the shadow of a tall building. Near his feet, broken glass. Just another drunk native. He had his hands tucked together between his legs, and you could see a couple of fingers sticking out the back near his crotch. Someone dead probably wouldn't cuddle his own hands like that.

I turned back to Daisy and had to blink a couple of times to remember why she was so pent up. "It felt like...," I said. "I don't know."

"He said something to you, didn't he?" Daisy said.

"What did he say to you?"

"Nothing really," I said. I was getting that feeling behind my nose, like when you're about to start crying. I held my breath so I wouldn't.

Daisy hit her two fists into the steering wheel. "Ugh! You *so* piss me off, Robin. You used to tell me everything. I tell *you* everything."

"I need a smoke," I said.

"Was it in English," she said, "or did he speak Tibetan? Did you understand him?"

I shook my head no. I wanted to say more, but my breath was still tied up in trying to hold back the pressure behind my eyes and nose. All I could do was mouth the words, no voice, just my lips shaping the words, "How the fuck should I know?"

I got out a cigarette and put it in my mouth unlit.

"Alright then!" Daisy yelled. "Just blow it out the window."

Daisy wouldn't look while I smoked, she kept her eyes straight ahead. She drummed her fireweed fingernails on the steering wheel. She was thinking that anyone stupid enough to smoke could at least smoke filters. I threw out my cigarette.

"Okay, I'll tell you what it felt like," I said. I leaned back, and put my feet on the dash. "If you're still interested."

Daisy blew the bangs off her forehead.

"Do you remember how we used to wake up in the middle of the night?" I said. "The sound of Mom and Dad fighting, before they split up? Remember how you'd get into my bed, and we'd put our foreheads together?"

Daisy bit her lip like someone on *Jeopardy!* trying to find the answer before the music stops.

"Like no matter how scary things got," I said, "no matter how scary, at least we were in it together?"

"Yeah?" Daisy said. "So?"

"So, nothing," I said. "So, forget it. That's kind of how it felt. No big deal."

"Did you see any colors?" Daisy said. "Did you see white light?"

"Nope," I said. "No white light." I got another Camel from the breast pocket of Les' workshirt.

Cold air came in through the open window. The shade of the tall building had spread and covered the car. It was only May, only warm if you were in the sun. The native had on jeans and sneakers and a sweatshirt. Not enough. He was still naked to the world.

"Pop the trunk for me," I said.

"What?" Daisy said.

"Pop the trunk," I said. "I need to get something."

I stepped out of the car and lit up. Took a long drag, then kicked shut the door. I went back and took the emergency blanket from the trunk. I walked over to the native. Dropped my cigarette, ground it out, and used the same foot to push broken glass off the curb. Then I opened the wool blanket and lowered it over his body. I watched his face in case he woke up. He had terrible skin, not scars like Les, just bad skin. His mouth was smushed open on the pavement and I tried not to look at his tongue hanging out. He had a clump of his hair stuck in the corner of his mouth. I saw the places where cold air could get in around his neck. I bent down by his back and tucked the blanket under his ear. I wanted to take the hair out of his mouth, but I didn't think a native would want anyone like me touching his hair, so I left it alone. I straightened up and got back in the car with Daisy.

I looked her straight in the eye.

"He called me Precious Jewel," I said.

"That drunk out there?" Daisy said. She looked out at the native and made a face.

"Sure, why not," I said. I smiled at my sister for the first time since who knows when. "I'll find you another blanket," I said.

"Don't worry about it," Daisy said, as she started the car. "Winter's over."

Blood and Roses

I first met Daryl in early spring while wandering the dry side of divorce. Lost in the high desert, I was following a trail of dust and rumors in search of the ruins of an old hot springs resort when I came to a broken stone wall on the edge of a dried up lake. A lavender school bus was parked by the wall, a bus with a sailboat for a roof.

I turned off the engine of my van and figured I must be somewhere.

Off in the distance, ranges and ranges of mountains. Nothing but rocks and dry dirt and cloudless blue sky. Yesterday was thirteen years gone wrong on the damp side of those mountains. Thirteen years married to a man with a low sperm count.

But that's not why I left. When Sam and I went to the fertility clinic and found out why I wasn't getting pregnant, we said we'd rather have a dog anyway. We brought home a puppy from the animal shelter and called her Baby just to lighten the mood, but the name stuck.

I knew what I was missing when I saw Sam with that dog. Sam in his easy chair with Baby's head between his legs and me alone on the loveseat pretending to read *The Sun* magazine, but the print had gone too blurry to read because it had been forever since I'd last heard Sam call me baby in that voice. I'd wished I had long floppy ears so someone would touch me like that.

And now here I was in this arid land, a place as barren as I was.

The engine ticked as it cooled. Wind slapped the van. My fingers uncurled from the wheel and I stepped out into a harsh sun. The ground was littered with shotgun shells and beer cans and plops of dried cowshit. Bits of green glass and black obsidian gleamed against the bleached alkali earth, and even though the sun was full force, the wind was cold at that elevation.

A woman up in the rigging on the lavender bus was trying to do something with the sails. Canvas snapped in the wind. Her balance seemed threatened by a heavy pile of dreadlocks. I squinted up and asked where I might find the hot springs. She pointed to a lone poplar that stood on the shore of the playa like an exclamation point.

I walked toward the poplar and found an algae-rimmed swimming pool surrounded by willow scrub and cracked cement. A handful of people wearing nothing but mud reclined around the edge. Their raccoon eyes watched as I bent to test the water.

"It's perfect," one said.

And it was. It was warmer than a womb in that slippery water. And when I was heated to the bone, the mud people offered me a drink of cold water they'd brought all the way from a spring on Mt. Shasta. They said I'd be purified. Then they showed me the swamp mud where the pool drained, and I stood there naked and let two women paint my body.

Mud nymphs, barely this side of girlhood, with young white teeth and bodies untouched by gravity. Free to squat and bend, they hid nothing as they covered me with warm mud pudding – my belly, my breasts, my thighs. I lay down on the cracked cement, a chrysalis under the sun, while the mud shriveled and dried to a pale sagebrush color. As it dried the mud came alive with needle sharp teeth. It pinched and prickled my skin until I washed it off in the pool's overflow. I went back in the water, pink as a baby.

That's when he came from below, circling my legs underwater. He swam like an otter, a sleek swirl of warm current around my knees, and then his face appeared, inches from mine, water streaming around eager green eyes.

Daryl.

The smooth skin of his chest, its slim growth of hair. He took a long look at me and then asked if he could float me around the pool. I closed my eyes and lay flat on the water and all I had to do was let go of my body, let warm water glide over my skin, let this strange young man move me in ever-slowing circles until there was nothing but the movement of water, its warm slow touch.

And hands, his hands under my shoulders and neck, the small of my back. His hands, their warm slow touch. Then after a spell, the hands were gone. The water was still and there was only my breathing. In and out. The gentle rise and fall of my chest.

When I finally lifted my head, the lavender bus was rolling across the playa, evening sun filling the sails, black smoke sputtering out the tailpipe. But what made my heart jump was the sight of one lone figure across the pool, his pack slung loose from one shoulder, a baby blue blanket draped over the other. I filled my lungs with air and dove deep to the slimy bottom. But I had to come up, had to open my eyes and look. And there he stood, naked and golden at the edge of the pool in that light. Naked and golden and grinning, so all he needed was a little flute and a set of horns poking through his tufted hair. And I knew who he was. I knew how it had to end

Still, I never meant to get pregnant, and Daryl promised he wouldn't come inside of me.

I know, I know. I'm an idiot.

And I saw the banality of our story even as Daryl stood there in that sunset light at the edge of the pool and said, "I was hoping to catch a ride with you."

"You don't even know where I'm going," I said. And hearing the flirtation in my voice, I knew exactly where I was going.

But no, not really. I didn't know what it was to hold a man inside me through the slow heat of an afternoon, until an owl suggests supper time and we notice our bellies are aching for food. I didn't know stillness or how you can arrive at stillness through motion. I didn't know you could wrap yourself around the entire planet and feel so vast that you hold all of existence inside, all that joy and suffering.

I didn't know I would come to worship God at the altar of sex.

***

That was spring, with the nectar of cottonwood buds drifting along the streams. By summer we'd moved high up into the canyon-fissured mountains, and now we were caught by October and Daryl's peyote was gone, along with the magic mushrooms and weed. And I had middle-age staring me in the face like a cold winter sun, but Daryl said women are like wine and I shouldn't worry.

I worried. My last two twenties broken on a bottle of tequila I never wanted in the first place and Daryl saying I should just cash out my portfolio because capitalism is a doomed system that's destroying the earth and why couldn't I just live in the moment. And then a mouse keeping me awake all night scrabbling around in my van, so close the sound seemed to come from inside my body. When I tried to tell Daryl he just wrapped himself around me tighter.

"Let it be," he said. "Go back to sleep."

No problem for him, his easy breathing in and out against my back. I guess they don't snore when they're that young, or lose sleep over things that gnaw in the dark – a mouse under the bed, financial matters, and that other nagging possibility. Why was I so late? Five, no six, six weeks without a drop of blood.

Moonlit boulders crouched in the sagebrush outside the wide open doors of the van, then faded to black as the half moon went down. I stayed like that, awake in Daryl's arms, fretting with fear until the stars drifted to nothing. The mouse finally quit whatever damage it was doing. When I could see the sun-streaked top of the distant rimrock I reached over the edge of the bed, got my sweatpants and hoodie off the floor, and tucked them under the covers where they chilled my belly while my backside reached into the heat of Daryl's body. Outside the top leaves of the aspen slowly kindled to bright yellow, and now my clothes were warm and the mouse was gone and surely my van was no more than a place to hunt crumbs in the dark. Surely my blood was no more than a couple of weeks late.

Daryl whined like an irritated puppy while I dressed beneath the covers, then grabbed my waist and tried to pull me back when I got out of bed. I worked my way out of the van, careful not to kick over the pee jar. The pee was covered with a crust of ice that shattered when I dumped it to the ground.

The card table under the aspen was piled with the dirty dishes I'd left to soak, now frozen in the pot. Also on the table a double-burner propane stove, a mason jar that held the thorny remains of a dead bouquet of wild roses, its water long since evaporated, and the half-empty bottle of tequila. What a mess. My fingers were almost too numb to strike a match. I tried to remember where in the van I'd stashed the gloves I hadn't needed since spring. I lit the propane stove and hoisted the pot of dishes on top. Gloves would make it hard to peel garlic or chop onions, but if I cut off the fingers I'd butcher a good pair of wool gloves. Did homeless people cut the fingers out, or did they find the gloves that way?

My icy hand crept down my pants in search of blood. I'd expected to bleed around the new moon, but that was almost two weeks ago. The night before we'd had a full-bellied half moon that poured out so much light I could have washed the dishes without a candle. I would have too, if Daryl hadn't started with that expensive bottle of tequila he'd talked me into buying on our last town trip. One hundred percent agave, he'd told me. For a special occasion. Then when the coyotes cut loose last night, Daryl decided we needed to celebrate the half moon. What was left of the bottle was sunlit amber on the messy table.

Any woman who might possibly be pregnant would never take hit after hit of hard liquor, would she? A nauseous tide rose at the thought of tequila. I closed my eyes and pulled my finger out from inside me. Promises to God, my last dollar on a box of condoms. I opened my eyes and rotated the finger before my face, wiped it dry on the sleeve of my gray hoodie, and studied the tight cotton weave, thread by thread.

A sound came from the van, Daryl was waking up. I put my finger into the pot of melting dishwater and hooked it to the handle of a blue enamel cup. Filled the cup with chunky ice water from a plastic jug and set it on the second burner. And now Daryl was growling and making stretching noises that made me want to rush to him like an animal in heat. His wake-up sounds alone were enough to make me forget how impossible our whole thing was.

And then silence again, but for the hollow rush of propane, its blue flame under the blackened pot, the sickness rising in my belly, the sun rising on the tequila. My last two twenties gone in that tequila, because I never say no to Daryl. Yes to leaving the dirty dishes. Yes to last night's drinking. Yes to the spell of firelight under the pagan moon, the scent of juniper wood, how it graces the night with its fragrance like temple incense. I couldn't have had enough tequila to make me feel so nauseous this morning, surely no more than one or two margarita's worth. Surely not enough to make me so queasy I had to grip the edge of the card table.

Daryl came up from behind and wrapped me in the wings of his baby-blue blanket. He pulled me to him, his hard-on lovely against my butt, the morning sun-glow in my eyes, and the world beginning to warm again. All I could do was fall into it all and let my head drop back on Daryl's shoulder as I offered my throat to the clear blue sky.

Daryl turned me around and put a warm wet kiss on my mouth. He had on my long purple skirt over unlaced hiking boots. No shirt, only his baby-blue blanket over his head, draped over his body like some Bible story saint. And his eyes as green and happy as summer. Eyes that didn't have it in them to see that summer is gone.

He took the potholder from the clutter on the card table and used it to lift the enamel cup off the flame. The potholder caught fire and Daryl dipped it into the dishwater. That potholder was part of a set I'd made to match the kitchen towels, no more than a sad reminder of a previous life.

"Winter's coming," I said. "We can't keep doing this."

"Yes we can," Daryl said. He spooned instant coffee into the cup, then pulled out a flask he'd hidden in the deep pocket of my purple skirt. He poured from the flask and stirred it all up, warmed his hands on the cup for a moment, then offered the cup to me, his green eyes full of giving.

So I drank from the cup, just to please Daryl. The heat of rum and coffee went down my throat to my belly. Then Daryl took the cup from my hands and raised it to the sunrise. Sunrise all over his uplifted face, sunrise golden on his chest and beard. Daryl bowed his head and touched the cup's chipped blue rim to his forehead before drinking.

With Daryl, everything is a ceremony.

Like the first time we made love, how he took my hand and led me through the sagebrush. Then he picked me up and carried me over the threshold of the stream to some grassy shade under the trembling aspen. And there was his baby blue blanket spread out and covered with pink petals, baby-pink rose petals, fresh and wild. Daryl must have spent the better part of the day wandering along the stream, gathering those petals from the thorny rosebushes that grew rampant among the willow and cottonwood.

But that was spring and by midsummer all the rosebushes along the stream were covered with plump shiny rose hips that, by now, had all turned the wrinkled color of dried blood. The grasses had gone to seed, and the stream was down to an easy step across. It wasn't that things weren't beautiful – the scattered aspen groves were temples of gold – but it was that desperate sort of beauty that wants to flaunt itself before it fades. You couldn't escape the fact that everything was changing.

"Daryl, it's getting colder every night," I said.

"We'll go to the hot springs," Daryl said.

I pictured the two of us neck deep in sulfurous water, surrounded by a dry swirling snow blowing across the desert.

"Let's go today," Daryl said. He drank down the last of his rum coffee, dropped the cup into the blackened pot of dishwater. "And tomorrow we'll head south." He picked up the bottle of tequila. "We'll spend the winter in Mexico."

"And use what for money?" I took the tequila from Daryl's hand and tightened the lid, then set the bottle down behind the pot on the table. I'd lost track of things, wasted propane, and now the pot was ready to boil. The dishes started to clink and clatter in there.

Daryl grabbed the tequila by its neck and headed off into the sagebrush. Daryl in my long purple skirt. Baby-blue blanket pulled tight around his back.

His back said it all.

Whenever there was something we needed to talk about.

***

Daryl and I didn't fight. Once, early on in the depths of a summer night, with Daryl on top and my legs twined over his, I'd softly asked him if he wouldn't mind washing the dishes once in awhile considering that I was the one who paid for and cooked all our meals. Daryl had stopped breathing, his entire body gone stiff. Except for his penis shrinking inside me. I'd held him tighter to my chest, squirmed my hips, and tried to bring him back to fullness. He'd pushed me off then and turned his back cold. He'd moved as far as he could to his side of the bed, then seemed to sleep peacefully while I spent the entire choking night trying to make a deal with God or the devil. Just to have Daryl touch me again.

The next morning I'd made pancakes while Daryl sat cross-legged and naked on one of the flat-topped boulders. Daryl naked in the summer light, his slender body open to the morning air, his back to me. I'd gone over and offered him a plate of pancakes and handed him a small jar with the last of my real maple syrup and because there was little left, I said he should take it all, I'd be happy to eat my pancakes with honey. Daryl had poured half of what little there was of the real maple syrup over his pancakes and handed me back the jar with the rest. I'd then looked into his eyes for the first time that morning and saw that he wanted me again, saw that I was forgiven. We'd left our pancakes to the flies and rushed back to our bed in the van.

***

Washing our dirty dishes that cold October morning, I would have bet my last dollar that this unwanted thing in my belly was spawned on that summer morning when I would have sold my soul to have Daryl love me again. The seed was planted and now this unwanted thing was trying to form itself into something wanted. Something soft and sweet with ten tiny toes and tiny fingers reaching and eyes as happy as summer. But no, a child needs a father, and Daryl was no father. Any fool could see that.

I left the washed dishes to dry in the sun while I went

hunting through the cardboard box of winter clothes under the bed. My wool socks were full of holes and dangly bits of yarn. My favorite red and pink alpaca sweater was eaten through the chest. Everything was sprinkled with mouse turds. I picked up a glove. A mouse hung by its teeth from the middle finger. A momma with a bunch of babies latched to her tits.

Kneeling there in the van, I held the glove at arm's length. The mouse hung on, and so did her babies. They were hairless and pink, with oversized heads. A thin membrane covered their bulging dark eyes. I jumped out of the van with the glove at the end of my arm, between the tip of my thumb and finger. I ran toward the stream and shook the glove, gently at first, then harder and harder, until the mouse finally flew off. She landed in a rosebush and tried to run to the ground, but her babies got snagged on the thorns. They wouldn't let go of her tits. She clawed at the branch. The harder she worked to get free, the more she impaled her babies on the thorns. They were torn and bleeding, their mouths wide open. The sound that came out was so tiny – almost beyond hearing. The mother jumped, and the branch dipped toward the ground, but she didn't have enough weight to fall free of her babies. Now she was upside down windmilling her feet into their pale little bodies. I squeezed my eyes shut, bent over and pressed my fists into my belly, as if that could change anything.

By the time I was able to look again they were gone but for one baby still stuck to a thorn. Its high-pitched cries drew me close. Transparent skin, one pinprick drop of bright red blood on its bulging belly. It had a beating heart and I couldn't believe the fingers and toes. I plucked it from the thorn. It slowly opened and closed its mouth as it curled in the palm of my hand, not much bigger than one of the shriveled rose hips.

I folded the waistband of my sweatpants to make a small pouch at my belly where I tucked in the baby mouse. Then I warmed some water on the stove, opened our last can of evaporated milk, poured some water into the empty maple syrup jar and added some milk from the can. I picked a loose bit of pink yarn from my shredded alpaca sweater and dipped the tip into the warm milk, then took the tiny thing from the pouch at my belly. I cradled it in my hand as I tried to coax its mouth open to receive a few drops of warm milk.

Grizzly Moon

This summer they'll be celebrating the sixty-year anniversary of the first time a man walked on the moon. Lydia from down the road told me all about it when she came to see me under the pretext of bringing me rhubarb pie. Lydia thinks it's her duty to check on me. She can't stop complaining that I'm too old to be living alone so far from everything.

Lydia said that Amazon will sponsor the biggest lunar laser light show of all time.

"That does it," I said. "I'm outta here." So Lydia said, "Where do you think you can go to get away from the moon?" I told her Alaska. She laughed like I was joking, then asked me if I remembered the first moon landing. "Sixty years ago is too far back to remember," I said.

As soon as Lydia went home, I stuck a For Sale sign out on the dirt road in front of my house.

The truth is, I do remember. I had just finished my first year of college and had escaped Texas to be a maid in Glacier National Park. And that was the night when, instead of going back into the dorms after our evening volleyball, all the hotel workers stayed outside with their transistor radios. This was back in another century, before cable or internet or cell phones, so there was no way to watch men on the moon if you were in the mountains of Montana. The other kids turned their radios up and pointed their fingers at the crescent moon. The noise of their cheering was like football season in Dallas, everybody getting all excited about this event that I had no feelings for. I remember the announcer on the radio, all wound-up, his voice covered with static, something about a giant step for mankind.

Well, I for one, have had enough of mankind and his giant steps. It seems he can't put his foot down without crushing the joy out of something. Like what they did to the moon. Today I'd wipe the sky clean of that blasphemous thing in a minute. But back in those days, it was the moon that lured you out into the night. It lit the Going-to-the-Sun Road and St. Mary Lake, which everyone said was the most beautiful lake in the world. That's what they told us at the orientation meeting. We were in the basement under the restaurant, the employee cafeteria, a bunch of college kids from all over the country. After the management had finished telling us how privileged we were to get jobs at the most beautiful lake in the world, a park ranger stood before us in his ranger hat and talked about grizzly bears. He told how they ate a couple of girls about my age. It all happened in one night, two grizzlies on opposite sides of the continental divide, each bear taking a girl out of her sleeping bag.

You can't help but wonder, what was the moon like *that* night?

Back then, they said the full moon could make you crazy. Nowadays it's supposed to make you go shopping. But what

I remember is how the full moon was a good excuse to party down by the lake, and it was Southern Comfort, not the full moon, that made me let the dishwasher, or maybe it was a busboy, let him stick his hands under my sweatshirt, until before I knew it, I was flat on the ground, with him on top of me. This guy I had no feelings for, trying to unzip my jeans. I said I needed to go to the bushes for a moment, and it was true, his weight heavy on my bladder. I squirmed out from under him and stumbled off into the aspen scrub. I pulled down my jeans and squatted there with my eyes closed. What a relief! The next time I opened my eyes it was to the sound of leaves shivering in a breeze. A thousand aspen leaves blinking at me in the moonlight. Nicer than any party, so I pulled my pants back up and glided along the lakeshore, away from the others.

And yes, St. Mary was the most beautiful lake in the world.

This was before the glaciers died. Before the blister rust and pine beetles and spruce budworm. Before the big fires.

Montana had it all over where I came from. Texas was too flat and Dallas was busy becoming the shopping capital of the world. My parents had made me get rid of my horse, Lightning, when the stable where I boarded him was bulldozed to make room for the new Sears. The abandoned cotton field where I used to gallop bareback was already under pavement when I left for Montana. And where I used to hear nothing but crickets, now it was nonstop freeway noise all night. But at Glacier Park, no cars were allowed in past sunset. Every evening the ranger came by and locked a gate across the Going-to-the-Sun Road. I'd walk past the gate, up the empty road, and the only sounds were the ones made by wind and creatures moving through the night. I gave it all my full attention, every little rustle, because that's what you do when you're in grizzly bear country. If a deer pulls leaves from a bush, you have to know what kind of animal is making that sound, and when you hear its teeth grinding the leaves, you see what happened to those two girls. You see moonlight on the slow curve of a claw, you see a girl's thin wrist flung across her pale moonlit face.

Still, every morning I finished my rooms in record time – no one stripped a bed faster or had a quicker hand with a toilet scrubber. I couldn't wait to put away my housekeeping supplies and slip out alone into the clean mountain air.

On one of my days off I hitched a ride through the Blackfeet Reservation to a northern outpost of the park, hiked into the backcountry along the Belly River, and then up a mountain beyond timberline. I found footprints in a patch of mud, tracks with the claw poking out a full finger length from the toe. I scanned a circle around me, then crouched down and fit three of my fingertips into the cold mud bowl of one toe. When I stood up my legs were shaking. My heart was beating so hard I was sure that bear could feel my chest pounding through the pads of its feet. Even as my mind raced along the miles back to the trailhead, my feet continued in the direction the claws pointed, up and over the next rise. Even now, pushing eighty, I still can't appease my hunger for seeing what's over the next rise.

There was the bear. Grazing on meadow grass, more like a buffalo than a girl-eating grizzly. A breeze lifted the hairs along the blond streak of its hump. Seeing the bear grazing turned out to be less alarming than not knowing where it was or what it was up to. Still, I backed off before the wind could turn on me.

All summer I'd been going in deeper and deeper, but that

time I went too far. It was getting dark, with no moon rising to show the trail out. I used the last of the daylight to find a backcountry ranger station that was marked on my map. The windows were dark and I hoped the door wouldn't be locked. Then I caught a whiff of cigarette smoke and made out the shape of a man sitting on the cabin steps. I knew I'd been spotted, but didn't break stride, just went on through the dusk-lit meadow, right up to the steps and told him I needed to borrow a flashlight, even though I really hate the way a flashlight spoils the night, how you can't see anything but what it's pointed at, and did he know, by the way, that there was a huge grizzly bear on that mountain behind his cabin?

His voice was low in the dark. "Yeah, I know that bear," he said. He said he'd welcome the company if I'd like to stay till morning. I considered the offer for a moment. Other than the cigarettes, he seemed more my type than the busboy or dishwasher.

He offered me a smoke. I told him no thanks and went on to let him know how much I hate the way cigarettes stink up the air.

"Well now," he said, "It looks like we've just met and already I've heard about two things you hate, so now I'd like to know two things you love."

"That's easy," I said, my eyes steady on the jagged edge between the mountain peaks and the stars. "I love being alone in these mountains, I love the way the air smells when you're up this high, and I love the moon when it lights my way."

"That's three things," he said. He held the cigarette out a distance from his face and said, "Do you want me to give it up?"

"What, smoking?" I said.

He nodded and I told him it's a free country, he can do whatever he wants, ruin his lungs, whatever, it's none of my business. "I don't even know you," I said.

He took a long, slow drag, then stubbed out his cigarette on the step and said that was the last one, he would quit forever. Then he went inside the cabin and got me his flashlight.

His name was Gordon. Gordon turned out to be the man who eventually, many years later, found me this place that I could afford to buy. That was back when Polebridge was still off the map, no more than a tumble of rough cabins along the Flathead River, without so much as plumbing or electricity. I loved the place for its access to the remote northeast regions of Glacier Park. Gordon would come shack up with me between his backcountry jobs, and it was on one of his visits that he told me about the Brooks Range in Alaska. He gave me a book about a woman who built a cabin in the Brooks Range all by herself. Gordon said she seemed a lot like me. Of course, as my too-close neighbor Lydia loves to point out, that woman was decades younger than me when she did it. But I don't care, they've still got a few grizzly bears and wolves up there. Gordon held firm he'd head for Alaska before grizzlies went extinct in the Lower 48. Well, they say that happened quite a while ago.

Extinct. What a word, unless you're talking about dinosaurs.

The Brooks Range. That's where I'm going as soon as I sell this place. I could have gone to Alaska with Gordon. He said I was welcome to join him, but I was mad that he was leaving, with or without me. I turned my back on him. We lost touch then, but I'm sure he made it. Gordon is a man who does what he says. Like with the cigarettes. I knew it was a lie that he was quitting on my account. I knew he said it like that to create something between the two of us. Still, even in spite of having quit smoking sixty years ago, Gordon might be dead by now. He was already in his twenties back in 1969.

That was before they let the local Blackfeet work in the park, back when it was all white college kids who got the jobs. Except for management, those geezers who left their Arizona retirements to come north and boss us around for the summer. They were maybe in their sixties, which seemed impossibly old at the time. But old age really isn't how you think it will be. I'm far older than that now and I still have the same feelings, still want the same things now that I wanted then, and that's why I've got to leave.

I'll escape Montana just like I escaped Texas.

And I won't let Lydia talk me out of it like she did last time when she drove me to town for supplies and I saw that new Dollar Store at the outskirts of Polebridge.

"See you in Alaska," I said, and I sat in the car and wouldn't set foot in that cussed place.

Lydia says I'm crazy to think of moving into the Brooks Range at my age. Lydia says I cut myself off from everything. She says if I'd just get cyberlinked then I'd be more in tune with the world, and I wouldn't take things so hard. Lydia says my going crazy that first time with the moon was my own damn fault, that it was all over the news for weeks before it happened. She says if I'm going to be so mule-headed about linking, then I should at least remember to listen to my radio once in a while, and not just to see if a blizzard's coming.

Well, I can't stand the noise of a radio. That's just the way

I am. I'd rather read if I want someone else's words in my head. And call me Auntie Diluvian, but I still read words printed on paper. That's what I was doing the evening they ruined the earth's one and only moon. I was reading a book, when suddenly there was a change in the light, something other than my lamp brightening the inside of the cabin. I looked up, and there was a glow out the window. It being the time of the new moon, that glow could only mean one thing, and this one thing filled me with the joy of a child at Christmas. I put on my parka and boots and I ran out into the snow. But it was not the northern lights, it was something else. It was slashes of light forming the letter M across the dark face of the moon. I stood there a long time trying to puzzle it out, and then I headed down the road to Lydia's.

Her husband was outside watching it too. He explained that it was all done with lasers and satellites. And no, he didn't think the moon should be turned into a Mega Mart billboard, but this was just the beginning.

"Wait'll you see what Pepsi's cooking up for the *full* moon," he said.

I clamped down on my jawbone and I restrained myself from cussing. He put his hand on my shoulder and said, "Maybe you'd best shut your blinds at night till you get used to it."

I took a step backwards, out from under his hand. "I don't want to get used to it," I said. "And my windows have never had *blinds*."

I stomped back up the hill, loaded my rifle, and emptied a few rounds at the moon. And now Lydia never misses an opportunity to bring up that story about how I shot myself in the foot, always using this little incident as proof for whatever point she's working on.

Like when she brought me the rhubarb pie and we took our plates and coffee outside and sat in the sun, and Lydia started in with, "I've been thinking about you…"

Watch out when Lydia says she's been thinking about you. What's next will be her instructions about how to improve your life. Sure enough Lydia goes on to tell me how she was in her garden cutting rhubarb stalks, which reminded her it was spring, which reminded her that spring is when I always take off into the mountains without telling anyone where I'm going or when I'll be back. Oh, I could see Lydia blazing a trail to my little mishap, and of course, she'd have to stop along the way to admire the view of herself roaring up to my cabin on her husband's snowjet to see what all the shooting was about, and how she found me bleeding to death in the snow.

Which is not at all how it was. That bullet barely grazed the tip of my big toe, and the only reason I wasn't back inside getting a Band-Aid was because when I slipped on the ice, not only did my gun go off, but I also fractured my ankle. So now, every time spring comes around, Lydia can't help but wonder what I'd do if something like that happened to me in the middle of god-knows-where. And it's no use reminding Lydia that I don't carry a gun when I'm out wandering, that will just set her off about all the other ways I could get myself killed.

So I took a bite of her rhubarb pie. I closed my eyes like I was in heaven. Then I told Lydia what a great cook she is, and how her kids must sure miss her great cooking now that they've all moved out. And how it looks like their loss is my gain. Well, that got Lydia talking about her kids for awhile, and then her rhubarb pie recipe. But soon enough she remembered why she came. She said that before I took off on foot anywhere, I had to tell her where I was going and when I'd be back. And I can see that this isn't a bad idea for a woman my age, but how can I do what she wants? How can I tell Lydia when I never even know myself where I'm going or when I'll be back? Even where it's burnt, the land is still lit with glory. Magenta fields of waist deep fireweed, pockets of cedar, hemlock, and fir that the fires missed. And the high country, where there never were enough trees to feed a fire, is about as good as ever, except for the missing glaciers and grizzly bears.

I try not to hold it against Lydia that she doesn't love what I love. She's like most of the others up here who breathed a sigh of relief when the last grizzly was air-lifted out. I've had skunks and pack rats live under my porch, so believe me, I know how it feels to want to get rid of something, even to the point of killing it. And maybe grizzly bears and cougars and wolves are no more than varmints, and maybe the moon is no more than a place to stick some company's logo. Maybe I'm no more than a deluded old woman who can't keep up with the changes. So I don't answer Lydia when she asks me why I go alone into the mountains. I don't tell her I'm searching for a footprint with the claw poking a good finger length out from the toe. I don't tell her that I need to prove them wrong about grizzlies being extinct from Montana. I keep my mouth shut. Because as much as Lydia says she cares about me, Lydia does not feel what I feel.

I don't tell Lydia I'm hunting for those feelings I had back when this was grizzly country. Those feelings as charged up and alive as when you're with a man, that strange mix of fear and excitement and yearning. Like the second time

I saw him, when I told Gordon I only came back to return his flashlight, but failed to mention that I chose the full moon to do it so I'd not feel rushed to leave. I handed him his flashlight and immediately rushed off to leave, before he could finish brewing me a cup of tea. I turned my back on him, my rule of thumb. I turned, and I felt him watching me walk away. Every step across that moon-sharp meadow took me farther from what I wanted. Until I was at the edge of the forest, and there it was – the bear crossing my path. It could have been a bear, or it could have been the shadow of a bear. I stood frozen on the edge for a spell, I stood there exposed under the cold bright moon. The man behind me, the bear in front, and me not knowing which one was making my legs shake, my heart thump. I took a step back, away from the bear, or the shadow of a bear, one slow step at a time. Then I turned back. I turned back and I rushed to the man.

He was still there, Gordon, waiting for me in the moon shadow of his cabin.

But now I'm on the far side of seventy and Gordon is gone. He's probably forgotten about me. He's probably dead.

Or maybe not. Maybe he went to Alaska, and maybe he made a life for himself in the Brooks Range, and one winter night he was drawn from his cabin by a strange light in the window, and he stepped out to look, and there was the moon at a time when the moon was not meant to be seen. Only it wasn't the moon. It was the letter M. And maybe he needs someone to hold him on the night of the Mega Mart moon, the Disney moon, the Nike moon. Especially in the dark of winter when there will be no sun to erase these terrible signs from the sky.

But come summer in the Brooks Range, the moon won't have a chance. The sun will be up all night, the bears will be out grazing with their cubs, and Gordon will want to share his good feelings with a woman who loves what he loves.

The Salvation of My Soul

I know you're wondering if I've got this beauty and the beast thing going with Bobby Dalfin. You wanted to hold your gaze steady, but seeing Bobby's face for the first time is like the part in the movie where you've got to shut your eyes. Then you had to pretend a sudden interest in his paintings on the wall. It's okay, Mike. You're only human, like all the other tourists who stop at our little roadside attraction. Some of them have heard about Bobby, some are here for his paintings, and some are just looking for an excuse to get out of their cars, what with being carsick by the time they come around that last bend. It's a narrow twisted road along this stretch of coast, and most days we've got rain and fog drowning out the scenery. The tourists can barely make out the words "art gallery" between swipes of the windshield wipers, but they steer toward the neon glow of those letters like seasick sailors heading for the harbor lights. And if Bobby's around, they'll be sure to slip in a word about motion sickness. The first-timers are ashamed of the looks on their faces. It's the parents who have the worst time of it, when their kid blurts out, "Why is that guy wearing a Halloween mask when it's not even Halloween?"

So here you are, Mike, and this is the place you read about in the *Living in Oregon* section of the Sunday paper. You saw my name and a picture of me in the shop with Bobby, his face respectfully out of focus in the background. Well, I understand your curiosity. It's not every day you see an ex-lover in the newspaper. And you just happened to be driving down the coast, a weekend getaway with—what's her name? Jenny? Your latest trophy, young enough to be a model. Oh, Jenny *is* a model and still in school. You're dating a high schooler? Okay, college. Whatever, Mike. I can hear it now, what you'll say to her when you two are safe in your car. My god, you'll say, that woman was up to six figures, and now she's making ugly baskets out of shriveled seaweed. And you'll hold out and make Jenny be the first one to say something about Bobby's face.

You're dying to ask, but you won't come out with it. *What's a woman like you doing with a man like that?* But you don't even know if we're doing it, and this is killing you. You and the entire citizenry of Alderville.

You look good, Mike, as usual. And I do too, now that you've had a moment to get used to my haircut. No, Mike, I haven't gone dyke on you. Why are you glad to hear that? And now that Bobby's gone to his studio, and Jenny's stepped out for a smoke, you want me to know it's not serious between you two. Jenny's not an *issue,* you say. You wonder if I ever make it to the city. Oh, I get it. This isn't about us, is it, Mike? This is about Bobby. I do believe you're offering me a mercy fuck.

You worked so hard at sex, Mike. Always a "ladies-first" man, except for that last time. I'm not mocking you,

Mike. Well, maybe I am. It's just that I never knew you well enough to tell you to stop. I'd open my eyes and watch you. Your face as tight as a fist. You never looked at me. And that last time! My God, the expression in your eyes when you finally opened them and got that I was dying. I'm sorry, I shouldn't laugh, but I've never seen you get off the way you did that night. It's okay, Mike. I'm cool with our ending. You couldn't have known what was going on. And I hoped that if I just ignored what was happening, that it would go away. Asthma's weird, and it can vanish as suddenly as it comes. But that night with you, it just got worse and worse and worse. I was an idiot, too embarrassed to say anything, until it got so bad I *couldn't* say anything, I could only try to push you off. And you growling in that sexy voice, "Fight me, baby, fight me!"

Please, Mike, don't apologize for abandoning me at the hospital. Why would you have stayed? So you could sit in a chair all night and fret over a woman you've never even had breakfast with? You're right, Mike, you could have called. But even if you had, it was over for me by then. And it wasn't just you. It was all the triple espressos, the closet full of empty wine bottles, the Valium disguised as vitamins.

Are you disappointed, Mike? Did you think I left town because you broke my heart? Sorry, I left Portland because I couldn't breathe.

This is where I come from. Breathing was never an issue for me here in Alderville. Then it was all about getting out of town before I turned into a druggie or got pregnant. Of course, I could always be saved by Christ.

Look, the fog's lifting. And Jenny's back from her smoke. She wishes she could afford a painting. Yes, Bobby's work is compelling, isn't it? She'll have to settle for one of my baskets. That one's made from kelp whips. I'm sure you've seen them on the beach, those big snarls after a winter storm?

And now the sun is out and Jenny thinks it would be nice for us all to go for a walk on the beach, her way of letting us know she's okay with our past, Mike. And with Bobby's face. No, Bobby won't come. I'll just turn off the sign and latch the front door. We don't need to drive anywhere, there's a path out behind the cabin. See where Bobby carved footholds into the cliff? Hold this rope and ease yourself down backwards. Grab the knots and your hands won't slip. Here, I'll go first and show you how easy.

We're in luck. The tide's out, and we've got the beach to ourselves. Are you sure Jenny's okay? Oh, she's just keeping her distance while she smokes. Well, that's thoughtful. Poor thing, listen to that cough. I'll never go back, Mike. I'll never go back to a place where I can't breathe.

And I thought I was suffocating in Alderville! I had to move to Portland to learn the meaning of the word. Here all I had to put up with was my mom and summer bible school and everybody's nose stuck in my business.

You should have seen me the year they made me Princess of the Rhododendron Festival. I was up high on the fanciest float in the parade, shivering my ass off in a tacky pink gown, and I'm looking down at the high school marching band and throwing soggy pink flower petals over the crowd. I'm wearing a rhinestone tiara and my best beauty queen smile, but what I'm thinking is, *I am so out of here*. And it wasn't because of the rain. Nine years out of ten it rains on the Rhododendron Parade, you expect that. What I didn't expect was how pissed-off I was up there, wondering what the hell is the use of being Princess of a trailer trash town like Alderville.

Jenny, you're back. Of course you can join us. I was just telling Mike about when I was a kid here. You're freezing, aren't you? Fleece doesn't help much when it's blowing like this. Here's a spot tucked into the cliff. We can get out of the wind. See, it's warmer here, even some dry sand. Mike was asking me why I came back to Alderville, but he's from New York, and if you've grown up with pavement under your feet you might not understand how it feels to be rooted in a place. But if you've got nothing but ocean in front of you and forest at your back, there's nowhere to go but outdoors. Especially if you're stuck with a mother who thinks you were spawned by the devil.

I'd escape from the house and spend an entire day reading in a stack of driftwood. Or snuggled up between tree knees, that's what I call those huge Sitka roots. I killed time with books, and I waited to start my life.

I finally got away, thanks to a fistful of scholarships. But I kept returning in my dreams. They were the kind of dreams you don't want to wake up from, the ones that feel better than real life. They'd start out in a forest. Sometimes there was a river with rapids, sometimes a slow stream with ferny pools. I'd get into the water and give myself to the current. I always woke up before reaching the ocean. Those dreams were how I thought sex was supposed to feel. They left me with a yearning that could never be satisfied by the grit-your-teeth performances of my waking life.

Ah, Jenny, you seem familiar with what I'm talking about. Sorry Mike, you want me to change the subject?

See that chunk of land jutting into the ocean? That's Cape Chinook, where I went when I got the urge to throw things at my mom. This is a woman who found tampons in my purse, then tried to haul me off to the clinic for a virginity check. I busted out of the car and took off running blind. Until I was like one of those dogs you see chasing seagulls. You know, when the dog's been held on a tight leash and suddenly it's free? I got to the end of the beach, and just kept going, right over the rocks and boulders. See that dark rubble over there at the bottom of the cliff? I was in some kind of zone, the way my feet glanced from boulder to boulder, no fear of slipping. All the way out to the end of the cape. I was up about fifty feet high with water around me on three sides, the tip of Cape Chinook towering behind me, nowhere left to go but into the ocean.

It would serve her right, I thought, to find my body washed up in a tangle of seaweed.

I heard a strange sound, a deep sucking of air from down below. My eyes followed the sound, straight into the blowhole of a whale. That wide-open hole felt like something I wasn't supposed to see. The hole closed and the whale went under. I couldn't wait around for the next breath. The tide was coming in. But it was already too late.

Well, obviously I made it back alive. But not until the next morning. Yes, a whole night out alone. No, you wouldn't die of fright, Jenny. You'd do what I did, try to make it back to the beach and when the tide cut you off, you'd look for a safe place to hang out until morning. And maybe you'd cry and maybe you'd yell, but eventually you'd pull yourself together. I worked myself off the rocks and up to a clump of trees at a break in the cliff, where I found a dry cubby in the tree knees. One night won't kill you, because even if you're cold and hungry and scared, at least you're not filling your lungs with salt water. I nodded off and woke up shivering cold. I smelled the resin from the trees, and

I listened to the surf crashing. I listened for the sound of a whale breathing. There were times throughout that long night when I thought I heard it. I felt, or maybe pretended, that the whale was nearby, keeping me company. I watched stars move across the sky, and eventually morning came. The tide was out, and I could go home.

My mother? She didn't believe me. To this day she's convinced I was with Vernon Russell. Vernon was Alderville's hotshot basketball player. Without Vernon, we never would have made it to state. He'd take possession of the ball and the crowd would go wild and I'd swell up with feelings about being his girlfriend. Until after the game when I was alone with Vernon. Then, whatever feelings I had about what was under those silky shorts evaporated like the mist off a broken wave. And there I was, the virgin princess. Stuck in a pickup truck on some logging road, pulling a hometown boy's hand out from under my bra and wishing I was home in bed with a good book.

My mother made me break up with Vernon after my night on the cape. She took one look at the twigs and spruce needles in my hair and said it was all the proof she needed that the devil had turned me into a slut. She said I wasn't allowed out after dark. I told her that was fine with me, thank you, I'd already fucked everyone there was to fuck in Alderville, and they were all pathetic. I told her she'd just saved me the trouble of having to give them seconds. And I got this spooky feeling she believed me. It was almost euphoric, what I imagine a surfer might feel catching a wave. I rode that wave. I told her, on second thought, they weren't *all* pathetic. I said Bobby Dalphin was pretty good, as long as I kept my eyes closed.

And I'm laughing now, but not just from remembering

the look on my mother's face. You should see yourself, Mike. I can almost feel your ears stretching to catch every word while you pretend to watch the ocean. And Jenny, you're wondering if you could ever do it with someone like Bobby.

I like you, Jenny. You're a lot nicer than I was at your age, but you attract men who think too much of themselves. It's what happens when you're too pretty. You scare off the ones who might really want to know you. Or want you to know them.

Bobby so desperately wanted me to know him. This was back when Bobby could talk, before his first operation. It was spring of my senior year—they let me skip my junior year. Bobby would have been a freshman, if he'd gone to school. He was home schooled, but Musetta needed help from tutors. Musetta was Bobby's grandmother, the one who fished him out of the creek when her daughter Doris tossed him in. Doris was still a teenager when she had this baby with a face she couldn't look at. I imagine folks told her she'd get used to it, but she gave up after a couple of months and threw Bobby into Alder Creek. Right after Sunday service, with half the town watching.

I was about three. I was busy watching the sun sparkles on the water. I saw Doris throw something into the sparkles. Musetta ran in, without bothering to take off her church shoes. The way she kept slipping on the slimy rocks, it looked like she was winding up to throw her purse. Then she fell, splat on her face. I wanted to play in the creek too, but my mom's fingers dug into me. She almost yanked my arm from its socket. I was crying and rubbing my arm, when Hattie North pushed her husband Pearly down toward the creek. Pearly got in and helped Musetta to her feet. Someone else fished out the baby, who was snagged on a log.

Everyone says it's a miracle Bobby didn't drown. He never even cried. And how the story grew, they said Bobby could breathe underwater.

Doris? She left town that day. They say the sheriff gave her plenty of time to hitch a ride out. Her mom raised Bobby. You wouldn't believe how many women get stuck with their daughters' babies in this town—it was my mom's worst fear. But Musetta had never finished high school herself. By algebra, she was out of her depth. My calculus teacher offered me extra credit to tutor Bobby. It wasn't so bad. We tried sitting across from each other on the table in the dining nook, but I couldn't read the numbers upside-down, so I had to sit next to Bobby. It bothered me some, how his eye could watch me from the side of his face. But I liked his voice. Bobby's voice came from deep in his chest. His mouth bent the words a little out of shape, but I understood most of what he said, and if I got confused about a word Musetta hollered it from wherever she was. Their trailer was that small. And it smelled awful from all the cats and dogs they kept.

Bobby was sharp. By our last session he was almost a grade level ahead of the regular freshmen, at least in math. And he had a better vocabulary than any of the other boys I knew. One new word I learned from Bobby was *cryptid*. Bobby showed it to me in a book. The book defined a cryptid as a creature whose existence hasn't been proven. Bobby was reading everything he could get his hands on about abominable snowmen and bigfoot. I had to follow him into his room, so he could show me his map of bigfoot sightings. Bobby's bedroom was hardly bigger than a closet. It felt like a girl's room, with a cutesy poster of a white unicorn surrounded by pink fluffy clouds. The unicorn's mane and tail looked like they'd been curled in a beauty parlor. The poster was full of rust-rimmed water stains and fly specks. The only furniture was a narrow bed and a dresser with a three-sided vanity mirror. The dresser was cluttered with plastic horses. I bent to look at the horses, and then checked out my face in the mirror. Just the right amount of makeup. And my hair was good from all three sides. Bobby's head was cut off, so you could pretend he was a regular guy in jeans and a sweatshirt. He was built more like a senior on the football team than a freshman. He told me the horses belonged to Doris. He said if she ever came home, she'd want her room back. That was fine with him, he'd sleep on the couch across from the TV, because everyone knows a girl needs her own room. I got the feeling that Bobby thought Doris was his sister. I straightened up and headed for the door, but Bobby wanted me to look at his map. I had to lean over his unmade bed and pretend to look at his map of Oregon, with its colored push pins, while my eyes were really peeking down at the dents his head had left in the pillow.

Next Bobby showed me a newspaper clipping about an elk hunter who claimed to see a sasquatch in the coast range behind Alderville. He showed me the red push pin on his map. Bobby said that was the first place he'd look as soon as he got his driver's license. He said if only he didn't have to wait that long. He said I was lucky to be able to drive. He said Musetta never drove him anywhere any more because her knees were shot to hell, so bad that sometimes he had to carry her to bed at night. Then Musetta pipes up from the other room that I should see how strong her Bobby is, he's the strongest boy in Alderville. I looked at my watch and said I had to go. As soon as I got home, I looked up the word cryptid, which wasn't in my dictionary, and abominable, which was.

There's Bobby. Do you see him? Way over there? I like to sit here, out of the wind, and watch him swim. That's true, people don't swim in this ocean, but Bobby's part sea mammal, I think. No, he wouldn't want to join us. He can't talk, you know, so what's the point? That's right, from his second operation. I'm surprised you know about that, no one talks about it any more, it was such an embarrassment to the town. No, I don't get the paper. I never saw the article. The reporter just asked me about Bobby's paintings, where he got his ideas, stuff like that. Oh well, I guess she snooped around town. Did the article mention Bobby's disappearance, his supposed suicide? I don't mind talking about it now, but I was as shamed by what happened as everyone else at the time. Especially the members of the fundraising committee and all the people who sent money.

I certainly didn't hesitate to send my check.

I remember when I first heard about the fundraising drive. I was in Portland eating breakfast in my riverfront condo on a Sunday morning, and there was Bobby Dalfin's face next to a bowl of strawberries on my kitchen table. The picture was taken outside Musetta's trailer. I could almost smell the mold and cat litter. The story promised a normal life for Bobby once his forehead was reduced and his eyes were moved and his nose and jaw were restructured. They even had a way to give him lips. Sure, I sent money. Someone mailed me a note saying Bobby would love to personally thank everyone who gave so generously, but the response to his story was so overwhelming that by the time I received this letter Bobby would be in recovery from his first operation. A year later I got a check from the Bobby

Dalfin Fund, with a short letter saying the surgery didn't go as planned, and Bobby was returning what was left of the money.

I got the rest of the story from Cheryl Wilson, an old classmate I ran into at the Lloyd Center. We chatted over coffee. Cheryl told me they only got as far as moving one of Bobby's eyes. It turned out he was in such constant pain they had to do brain surgery. After that he couldn't talk, and he was still prone to killer headaches. He had to quit his job sorting mail at the post office. Then Musetta died, and Bobby disappeared. Everyone figured he killed himself. And folks in town didn't mention Bobby anymore.

They sure missed seeing *my* face though, Cheryl said, and why didn't I ever come home? Cheryl told me who all had gotten fat since high school, and how many kids they had, and how the whole town was on food stamps since the mill shut down. I was only half listening. I was thinking about Cape Chinook.

Look at the size of those waves crashing against the tip. Can you make them out through the mist? Cape Chinook was as alive to my senses in that Portland shopping mall as it is right now with us looking at it. I almost asked Cheryl if they'd thought to look for a body along the bottom of the cliffs. Had they searched all the way out to the end of the cape? Then I remembered the whale, how close we came to each other, the sound it made sucking all that air into its lungs. No, I didn't want anyone else going out there, ever. That was my place, and if Bobby ended his life there, then it was his place too, and it all deserved to be left alone.

Cheryl was going on and on about the Rhododendron Festival. She said she was on the parade committee, and how hard it was to find a decent princess these days, so many of the girls were either fat or in therapy for bulimia. She said she'd caught her own daughter, barely thirteen years old, sticking her finger down her throat over the toilet. And what did girls these days have against staying healthy? So I leaned across the table and said Cheryl, listen to this. I gave her a demonstration of my wheezing. She said it sounded like someone playing bagpipes inside a pillow. This is nothing, I said, you should hear it when I lie down. Nights are hell. Asthma is a stalker who sneaks into your dreams and pulls a curtain down on you. You can't breathe. You're gasping for air. You're trying to claw your way out. The nightmare goes on and on and on. Until you finally wake up and realize you're in the throes of another asthma attack.

I remember, Mike, how you once said it was a breath of fresh air that I didn't make you cuddle with me after we did it—you're okay with this, Jenny?—but I was afraid to fall asleep in any man's arms for fear of being seen like that.

Yes, Jenny, I tried acupuncture. Along with anything else you could name, but the treatments wouldn't keep. I hung on for a few years, until one night I almost died. Mike was with me when that happened, he's the one who took me to the hospital. That's when I remembered something Cheryl had said to me that afternoon at the Lloyd Center. Cheryl said I was probably allergic to the air in the city. She said I should try coming home.

So I did. I came back in the spring, when the creeks were in flood, and the alders along their banks were like clouds of green mist. But my mother was still my mother, and even worse, I was still her daughter. She still muttered to Jesus about how I let the devil have his way with me, and when was the last time I'd been inside a church. All this under her breath, like someone talking about you behind your back, but never a word about my promotions or the stocks I'd bought in her name or the upgrade to her health insurance. And you know me, Mike, I am the epitome of cool with obnoxious lawyers and meddlesome shareholders, but this simple-minded woman had me screaming curses at her within days of my return. She grabbed my arm and dug in her fingers, the same as when I was a little girl and tried to follow Musetta into Alder Creek.

Back then my mom said Bobby was Doris' prize for her sin. Well, I thought a prize was what you got at a birthday party. A prize could make you forget that your arm still hurt where your mom yanked it. I crept in through everyone's legs, and there was the wet baby in the grass. The grownups were in a circle like trees blocking the sun. They wagged their big slow faces back and forth and whispered things to each other. I touched a finger to its open little hand. Its tiny fingers curled shut around my finger and pulled my finger into its mouth. Inside that mouth was as warm and wet as a puppy. The baby sucked hard on my finger, but then my daddy picked me up and carried me off. He set me on my feet under a lilac tree and told me to stay put, then he walked away. We never saw him again.

Over the years I developed the same idea for myself. As soon as I was old enough, I'd walk away and no turning back.

But here I was at age thirty, back in Alderville yelling at my mother to go fuck herself. I pulled my arm free of her pinching fingers, threw some stuff in a backpack, and stomped up the beach. I sat in a pile of driftwood and waited until the tide was out, then worked my way along the edge of the cape. By sunset I was climbing up to the spot where I'd been forced to spend the night when I was a girl. A blue plastic tarp was strung between two giant spruce trees. Someone else was camped there. I looked down, and already water was swooshing over the same rocks where moments before I'd been walking. I searched around the edges of the campsite for a way out, but it was all black cliffs above and raging ocean below.

That's right, it's easy enough for you to figure out whose camp it was, but at the time everyone thought Bobby was dead, and we *wanted* him to be dead. Don't look at me like that, I'm only telling you the truth. I figured it out when I was three years old. I turned from watching my daddy walk away, and I saw it then, how they were all afraid to look at Bobby now that he was alive. They acted so sad when they thought he was drowned. They all stared down at his limp body, shook their heads, and said it was too bad. Until he grabbed my finger and started sucking. My dad picked me up in his arms, but I saw their faces over his shoulder. I saw their tight-lipped looks. I saw how some of them wanted to yell at me.

From then on, I saw Bobby like everyone else did. And I sent my check to the Bobby Dalfin Fund.

Bobby came down from the tree where he'd been hiding. He was taller than I remembered, and bald, and one of his eyes had been moved from where it used to be. He was dressed like the winos in old town Portland, with duct tape wrapped around the toes of his sneakers. But his camp was decent. He had hundreds of empty mussel shells stacked in neat piles. Sinuous pieces of driftwood were arranged like a sculpture garden. The setting sun streaked in between the tree trunks and lit up a pile of agates. It seemed they were placed just so, to catch those last rays. So it was only Bobby, and not some slasher rapist I was trapped with. I said I was sorry to invade his space, but I couldn't leave until low tide. And now it was getting dark, so where should I put my tent?

That night my tent kept out the wind and the rain, but every so often I heard Bobby's blue tarp rustle. I didn't know if it was him moving around in there or wind making those noises. I tried to figure out what to do about my mother, and what to do the next day, and what to do with the rest of my life, but the booming surf made it hard to think. Eventually I quit trying. It was cozy in my sleeping bag, while outside was fierce wet commotion.

And I could breathe. No night stalker came to sit on my chest and crush the air out of me.

The next morning I tried to give Bobby my food, I had enough for a week, but he wouldn't take it. I told him he was crazy not to, he must be sick of mussels. I went to take down my tent. Bobby's foot came down on the stake when I bent to pull it. I looked up from his duct-taped shoe, and he shook his head. He swept an arm around the campsite. "Are you sure?" I said. He nodded vigorously. "Okay, then," I said. "I'll stay awhile longer."

Bobby showed me how to get past the cliffs and into the forest, even when the tide was up. As the days warmed up and got longer, I spent less time sitting by the fire and more time exploring elk trails and tidepools. I found the spot where seals came out on the rocks to nap. Sleeping, they looked like a cluster of giant slugs. It was hard to watch them drag their smooth bellies across the jagged rocks. They seemed like big fat mistakes when they were out on the land. One day it occurred to me that I didn't know what those seals were feeling. I only knew how it would feel if it were me. That evening Bobby dropped mussels into the pot of boiling water, and I wondered what *they* were feeling. I wondered if Bobby had any idea how like female genitalia those mussels looked when they opened wide and revealed their swollen parts. Not to mention the smell. I figured Bobby was the only man I knew who wouldn't look into my eyes, or do something suggestive with his tongue, when he put one of those slippery things in his mouth.

I ate my backpacking food and shared it with Bobby. After awhile I ate whatever he cooked over the fire. Fish, kelp, nettle. Eventually, even mussels. And every evening I crawled into my cozy sleeping bag and felt the air flowing in and out of my lungs, and when the tide was out, I listened to the wind in the trees. It was a sound as deep and easy as breathing.

The weather? You know Oregon, but we stayed dry enough. Rain squalls were constant over the ocean. I'd see some dark turbulence moving toward us, and I'd scurry around picking things up. Usually by the time I had everything under cover, the column of rain would have turned elsewhere.

One day I was watching the sky, and I mentioned this to Bobby, how little rain we got, considering what was going on all around us. He came over with his worn spiral pad and squatted beside me. He drew a quick pencil sketch of Cape Chinook. He sketched my tent and his tarp. He drew arrows in the ocean and arrows in the sky, all aimed at the cape, but with the points curved away from our campsite. I asked Bobby if the arrows were currents of wind and water. He nodded. He sketched trees on the cape, windbent and hugging the ground. On our campsite he drew the trees straight and tall. I told Bobby it was a good sketch, better than anything I could ever draw. He flipped to another page and showed me a bald eagle rising from the water. The eagle had a dripping fish in its talons. I recognized the estuary a few miles to the south. I knew it was the estuary from the reflected snags in the water. The closer I looked, the more shadowy shapes I saw under the ripples. I saw a baby under the water. I saw the suggestion of a naked woman. I told Bobby he was an artist.

Yeah, you could say I discovered Bobby.

I reached out for his book, I just wanted to look at the rest of his sketches, but he clutched it to his chest. That's when I got the idea that maybe he had some drawings of me in there. I left him alone then, and I wandered into the woods. I came to a certain place in the forest where moss covered everything, a place where the very air seemed lit with green fire. I pressed my body into the moss. It yielded like the deepest down comforter. I pushed my nose into the moist smells. I thought about you, Mike, and I thought about Vernon Russell in his silky basketball shorts. I remembered all the men who had ever put their hands on my body. And I wondered if Bobby was hiding somewhere in the shadows, watching me. I wondered if Bobby was bringing me to life in his sketches. I lay in the moss, and I imagined an artist's eye on me. I couldn't picture the artist's face, but he had a lean, muscular build like Bobby's. I started to touch myself. I heard my mother screaming at me, screaming that I was a dirty little girl, my mother digging her fingers into my arm, yanking my hand away from the warm soft place.

I've never told this stuff to anyone. Should I go on? You sure? Okay.

So. That same afternoon I undressed out in the open, instead of hiding behind the rocks like I usually did. I took off my clothes by the stream near our camp. I rinsed them and spread them to dry. I felt every muscle. Each move I made was a pose as I balanced on the rocks and bathed. I came out dripping and arranged my body on a flat rock in the sun and I thought, well, maybe Bobby's watching, and maybe he'll draw me.

You can relate to this, right Jenny? Yeah, Mike told me you're a model.

Well, Bobby never showed up that evening. I'd thought I was doing him a favor when I gave him a chance to see my body, but by sundown I was thinking I'd made a big mistake. And the more I thought about it, the more wrong I felt, because if it was not an invitation, then it could only be a tease. And what kind of a woman would tease a man like Bobby, and what kind of girl would wiggle around on her daddy's knee and let him put his finger in her warm soft place, so that he would have to leave home and never come back.

All night I lay awake in my tent. I listened for the rustle of Bobby's tarp, but the ocean was all I heard moving. I fell into a dream world shrouded in moss. I tried to thrash my way out, but the moss covered my mouth. The moss covered my nose. When I finally broke through the moss, it was to the suffocation of an asthma attack. The ocean was too close. The air was congested with its roar. I sat up and wanted to scream, but screaming needs breath, and all I could do was hit at the sides of my tent. An arm reached in, and Bobby pulled me out. He propped my body against a tree. Something pushed hard into my chest. And then it was over. I coughed a few times. I breathed in and out. The ocean sounded right again, and I opened my eyes to the reflection of moonlight on Bobby's bald head. Bobby's head was between my bare breasts. He was on his knees in front of me, pushing his head hard into my sternum. I understood that what Bobby was doing had stopped the attack. I lifted my face. I watched tattered clouds crossing the moon, while my fingertips felt the scars where someone had cut into Bobby's skull. I asked him if he still got the headaches. His head moved between my breasts, and I understood that to be no. And I was so glad, so suddenly free of myself, that I didn't mind the sharp spruce needles poking my skin as I stretched out naked on my back. They only added to the proof of what Bobby and I were doing, proof that I was alive, proof that I was finally able to feel something.

I kept my eyes open while we were wet and warm inside each other, and Bobby's one good eye never left me. And the ocean rose and fell under the moon.

I followed Bobby around all the next day. That's how I found out he was swimming in the ocean. His head stood out, slick and hairless and pale. The seals in the water around him were watching me. I stepped into the sparkles on the water. The ocean tugged at my ankles as I watched Bobby swim.

I hope those tears aren't on my account, Jenny. I've never been better. The asthma's gone. I'm where I want to be. Are you?

Yeah, Mike, he did draw me. No, those aren't in the gallery.

How'd we end up back in town? Someone reported a sasquatch sighting on Cape Chinook, and we had an invasion of cryptid hunters. We hid from them, but they found our camp. We fixed up Musetta's rundown old doublewide and stayed there until I bought the gallery. It's perfect for us, with its studio and cabin out back.

I returned to my mother's house once to ask her where my father was. She didn't know and didn't want to know.

She said he was gone and good riddance. He left town with Doris Dalfin the day she threw her baby into Alder Creek. She said my father was the devil himself when it came to young girls.

I have no answer for that question. Maybe Bobby's my brother, or maybe my dad just saw Doris on the side of the road and gave her a lift out of town. Someone saw him pick her up, and that's as much as we know. It's possible that my mother knows, but she keeps her thoughts to herself these days. We have her over for dinner most Sundays after church. She never goes off any more about the salvation of my soul.

Naked Glass

We were still in shadow and frost under the pines, while the forest across the river was lit with sunrise. It was awfully early to see people on the other side, usually it was just birds and animals at this hour. But there they were, two humans, a man and a woman. And, for the life of me, they weren't wearing a thing! A naked man and a naked woman in my floor-to-ceiling picture window. They stood there by the water in front of the broken-top ponderosa, its mammoth trunk bright orange, their skin a smoother reflection of sunrise.

My tea water started to hiss. I backed away from the glass into the kitchen, and was once again surprised by the face wrapped around the teakettle. All wadded up, a cartoon picture of old. The hand that took the kettle off the stove was as old as the face. It still comes as a shock, this business of aging. But I mustn't complain. At least I don't have arthritis or cancer or Alzheimer's or you name it. I'm one of the lucky ones, bless my heart.

What was the word Jack used the other day at the museum?

Spry.

Of course, it takes two cups of Earl Grey to even approach spry. I took my tea to the breakfast bar, where I keep a good pair of bird-watching binoculars. The naked man and the naked woman were even more naked with their arms raised to the sky. I could see everything, the shine on their ribs, their armpit hairs, and a whole lot more that I probably shouldn't have looked at.

I put down the binoculars, tightened the belt around my quilted housecoat, and tiptoed to Howard's door. Howard was still asleep and snoring, making a muddy noise that made me want to hold my nose and keep moving. Time was, I didn't mind when my husband snored. That raw male sound made me feel all the more female.

Bless our hearts, nowadays Howard's snoring means separate bedrooms.

***

The naked man was filbert brown all over, while the woman was honey gold. Her hair was cut short like a boy's. She was a blonde, but amber-colored down at the patch. His hair was black in both places.

They jumped into that fast Deschutes River as carefree as frogs. She swam a champion crawl, but all her stroking just held her in place against the current. Meanwhile the man was swept against a big drift log. He hoisted himself out and lay there, his belly flat over the log's white curve. Steam rose off his back. His bottom was as dark as his arms and legs.

From down the hall, I heard the shower door slam. In my mind's eye, I saw the door slowly swing back open and Howard's arm come from the steam to catch it before it could arc out of reach. Then the click as he shut the door properly. Every morning Howard forgets that if you slam the door it will only bounce back open.

Every morning. Slam, pause, click.

Outside, the naked woman was still in the water. But tiring against the river, you could see. Her armstrokes less vigorous, her mouth wide for air with every stroke. She was moving backwards, closer to the log and the naked man on the log. He was as still and brown as those plaster Paiutes at the museum where I work.

The shower went silent. When Howard came into the kitchen I made sure I was at the sink washing my spoon and cup, but I needn't have worried about him looking out the window. Howard wasn't interested in the river, or the forest on the far side of the river. In his old burgundy bathrobe, Howard was a study in slumpage. Shoulders, donut belly, jowls. He poured a packet of hot cocoa mix into a fat cup, then added a spoon of instant Folgers and hot water from the teakettle. He stirred it, sloshing chocolate powder on the tiles. Then he left the kitchen without lifting his slippered feet, head bent down to his cup, as if a close watch could slow its wave action.

I followed with a sponge and blotted his spills off the rug.

Howard sat with his back to the window. His back to the river and the naked man and the naked woman. Howard sat facing his television, remote in hand, and, bless his heart, this is how my husband will be for the rest of his life. Knee replacement, back surgery, triple bypass. Not all at once, but over the years. He never said a word when I moved his golf clubs from the entry hall to the attic in the garage. I brought home books. Steinbeck and Jorge Amado on the glass coffee table where Howard puts his feet to watch television. *Best American Short Stories* on the windowsill in the bathroom. I had the library special order *The Old Gringo* in large print.

As if making the words bigger would make Howard want to read.

The library was where I saw the notice asking for volunteers at the Oregon High Desert Museum. The poster showed a side view of a kestrel, its talons wrapped around a man's gloved wrist. The man looked like he fed on the same diet as the bird. Insects and sparrows and lizards. With a face he'd forgotten to bring in out of the wind and sun.

Jack.

***

I wiped more spilled cocoa off the kitchen floor, then washed out the sponge. Back behind the breakfast bar, I picked up the binoculars. The naked woman was still in the water, her arms on the white log. Even on the hottest summer day, it takes every ounce of courage for me to dunk in and out of that icewater. Up where we live, it's still too fresh off the mountain to be tolerable. It's not until the Deschutes winds its way through a few desert canyons that it even approaches swimmable. But there she was, on a chilly September morning, in up to her neck. She shot up like a fish and struck at the man's rear end.

I let out a sound like someone's teeth had bitten *my* rump.

The TV went silent. "Ellie?" Howard said. "Babycakes?"

I lowered the binoculars and turned. On the screen wet girls bounced up and down in red and yellow bikinis under a postcard sky. Their arms pushed Pepsi through the screen and into my home.

"Are you okay?" Howard said.

"It's nothing, sweetheart," I said. "Just a red-breasted sapsucker."

The sound came back on. For once, I was glad to hear

that noise. Through the binoculars, the naked man and the naked woman were both in the water now. She was on all fours trying to crawl onto the shore. He put his hand around one of her ankles and pulled her back in. Next came a lot of splashing as they slapped water into each other's faces. And then, just how animals do, they stopped playing as suddenly as they'd started, and they got out. They stood serene and dripping, everything bare under the sun.

I pulled up a bar stool and rested my elbows on the counter. Those binoculars were too heavy for my wrists. I'd bought them as a retirement gift for Howard when we moved into this house.

As if making the world bigger would make him notice.

Like the time I saw a merganser come down the rapids with her train of yellow ducklings. And one baby duck, out of the train, who rode high and dry on top of her back.

Howard didn't bother to focus.

Then there was the bear. Now a swimming bear, that's something! I was on the deck watering geraniums, and I shouted for Howard to come see, but he had the TV so loud he didn't hear me. The bear did though. It turned around midstream and swam back to the far shore, then shook itself off like a dog and ran into the pines.

Even after the bear, I never once saw Howard pick up the binoculars on his own.

The naked man lifted his arm and pointed to the sky. I followed his finger up to where an osprey flew over with a fish in its talons. The fish sparkled silver against the bird's white belly. The nest was on my side of the river, a big sloppy pile of sticks on top of a snag that rises over the rust-green forest. You could see the nest from the far edge of our deck, but not from where I was inside the house.

I watched the naked man and the naked woman watching the osprey.

***

Howard would have bothered to focus for the naked woman. I ought to have let him in on that. But wasn't it always the same, every time I tried to bring him in? The yellow merganser chicks weren't so yellow once they'd had a chance to bore Howard. And the bear turned into something he needed to go out and buy a gun for.

No, best leave Howard out of it. One look at the naked man's dingus and he'd turn it all into something involving the sheriff.

The naked man stood no taller than the woman beside him. A short man with a long dingus. I fine-tuned the right lens focus. I suppose height's got nothing to do with it. Howard used to stand a good six two. Time was, his chin was a perfect fit over the top of my head.

But then there was the naked woman. How many more chances would a man like Howard have to see living nipples as fresh as hers? And in all fairness, Howard was the one who bought me all this. This house. This view of the river with the Deschutes National Forest on the other side. No worry that we'd never be bothered by the sight of someone else's house outside our picture window.

And, bless his heart, Howard *was* getting better about remembering to mute the commercials.

Still.

***

Skim milk, two ripe bananas, nonfat yogurt, strawberry flavored protein powder, blender, two mugs. I brought it all over to the breakfast bar. The naked man stepped into a pair of loose lavender pants, no underwear. I peeled the two bananas and put them in the blender. The naked woman held up a breezy length of peach-colored fabric and shook it out in the wind. She spent some time artfully wrapping it around her body. I poured milk, added yogurt and protein powder. He helped her tie the wrap over one shoulder. They rolled up their sleeping bags and held hands as they walked off barefoot beyond the broken-top ponderosa, intimate with the whole living world.

I turned on the blender. It made more noise than the TV. I filled the two mugs and took them to the glass coffee table in front of Howard.

"Thanks for the bacon and eggs," Howard said, without taking his eyes off the TV.

Thanks for the bacon and eggs is what Howard says every morning. Ever since his cardiologist said no more bacon and eggs.

I sat with my back against the armrest of the sofa, facing Howard. "Just the way you like 'em," I said. "Crisp and over medium."

Every morning, whether it's granola or oatmeal or smoothie.

We drank pink smoothies, and I watched Howard watching *Good Morning America.*

***

Driving to work that day, through the pines and sagebrush, I had the naked man and the naked woman tucked into the corner of my mind where I keep the list of things I plan to tell Jack. The mergansers, the swimming bear, the time I saw a giant condor in Peru. I could start by mentioning the osprey with its fish. That way if Jack took the naked man and the naked woman the wrong way, I'd have the osprey to fall back on.

Truth be told, birds were about the only thing I knew about Jack.

The only times I spoke to Jack were when he'd come over between his raptor talks. He'd lean into the counter like some skinny old cowpoke in a saloon. "So how's my best gal?" was the usual opener. His elbow on the polished wood, his body angled so he could keep one blue eye on whoever was coming in from the hot summer light. Parents and children looking for the restroom. Teenage girls in clothes that left no room for doubt. Old folks who'd gone beyond caring that Bermuda shorts let everyone see the wormy purple veins on their legs. His other blue eye kept watch on the entire summer sky, which according to Jack, was as full of identifiable life as the museum lobby.

"Immature peregrine," he'd say, like he was talking to himself.

Or "Golden eagle. Male. Riding the thermals. And another one higher up, must be his wife." As if these things were as common as cars on the highway.

"Where?" I'd say, and if I wasn't busy answering some tourist's question, I'd look near and far, high and low. Anxious to not miss something good, I always missed it. Or saw no more than a speck moving beyond the tree line. Perhaps eagle, but for all I could tell, it could have been buzzard.

Truth be told, when I first started at the museum I suspected Jack of fabricating birds out of the blue. Until the time Jack said, "Prairie falcon fixing to nail someone."

"Show me!" I said. It must have been something in my voice, because Jack drew his entire attention away from the sky. He gave me a look, his eyes a caricature of wide open, while his mouth held down a grin. He came around to my side of the counter, and he put his face down alongside mine and stretched his long arm with its finger pointed. Sure enough, there off the tip of his finger was a bird flapping its wings over a juniper, as awkward as treading water. Then it went down feet first into the rough green of the juniper and came right back up with something limp in its talons, something that dangled a fuzzy tail.

I never saw what happened next. A boy wearing a headset, along with a face to let the world know he'd been forced to attend family vacation, was asking me if there was anyplace he could buy batteries. I pointed him in the direction of the gift shop. Right behind him were some Germans who wanted to see buffalo.

I had to tell them we didn't have any buffalo, that this area had never been buffalo habitat, but I was sure their children would enjoy the otter exhibit. All they had to do was just go out that door over there and follow the path, and they'd find the otters on their left, just past the covered wagon.

By the time I got through explaining that Oregon is not all rain, and that, as far as I knew, this wasn't where someone had gotten rabies from a chipmunk bite, but it's still best not to feed or touch wild animals, Jack was long gone, and so was the falcon.

But now that Labor Day weekend had come and gone, things would slow down at the museum. Already the world was changing. Our side of the river stayed cold in the shadows a little longer every morning. A certain yellow color to the light, even as I pulled into the museum entrance at noon. The familiar panic that goes back to every September for as long as I can remember. The one where summer is ending, and I still haven't done the things that I wanted.

I parked the car where I always do, facing the gray skeleton of a dead juniper.

For the life of me, I'm not ready to be this old.

***

Most of the visitors were either outdoors or in the auditorium watching the slide show. I was picking up abandoned brochures from the front counter when Jack came in through the glass doors that lead to the raptor rehabilitation center.

"That Lilith is the angriest bird I ever had to put in a cage," he said. The sleeve of his khaki shirt was slightly torn with few spots of blood. He rolled it up past a small puncture a few inches above his wrist. "Most birds just get depressed," Jack said. He looked down on his wound, then pushed aside the bulky guest register and leaned across the counter, so close I could have counted the white neck hairs he'd missed shaving. "I don't suppose you'd be willing to spare an injured man a kiss or a Band-Aid?" he said.

A lifetime of flirtation behind the serious in those blue eyes.

And I'm one of those people trapped in the kind of skin that shows everything. The first aid kit was under the counter, I knew exactly where, but opened all the wrong doors. I knew better than to take Jack personally, and yet, for the life of me, I couldn't stop the silly pink flush that I knew was spreading all over my face.

I finally came up with the blue box. Jack set his arm before me on the polished wood. The blood was only on his shirt, just a small stain. His arm was full of scars and ropy muscle. Jack's arm looked as abandoned to the weather as his face, and so brown I had to wonder where his tan line would be. On up where a T-shirt sleeve might end? Down around his waist? Or maybe Jack was like the naked man by the river, all one color, no line at all. I'd only seen Jack in the long-sleeve shirts and blue jeans he wore at the museum.

Jack could be anything.

I made a point of paying attention to what was needed from the first aid kit. Hydrogen peroxide, cotton balls, anti-bacterial ointment. I cleaned the puncture with a peroxide-soaked cotton ball, then moved to put my other hand on Jack's wrist, but fanned the air with it instead. "This should stop foaming and dry a bit before we cover it," I said.

His eyes still rascally on my face.

"She bit you?" I said. "The great horned owl?"

Jack's head moved up and down, but his eyes stayed steady on mine.

"Lilith," I said.

Eyes like he knew something.

"That's a pretty name," I said.

"Lilith was Adam's first wife," Jack said. "Refused to let her old man boss her around."

I squeezed ointment onto a Q-tip and touched it to the wound. "This looks about right, don't you think?" I said, holding up a medium size Band-Aid.

"I heard it said that if you sleep next to an owl feather you can see and hear what other folks are trying to hide," Jack said.

"My husband doesn't boss me around," I said. I tore open the paper around the Band-Aid.

Jack turned his head and looked out at the sky through the glass wall of the museum. "Juvenile red-tail," Jack said. "Looks to be female."

Pressing the Band-Aid to his skin, the warmth of Jack's living flesh came up through my fingertips. You wouldn't expect something so hard and tough to be warm. I rolled down his sleeve and buttoned the cuff. Then patted the back of his hand and said, "That's a small enough rip in your shirt, it'll be easy to mend. You should probably go wash off the blood before it sets."

Jack tipped an imaginary cowboy hat. "Thank you, Ma'am, I'll do that," he said. On his way to the men's room, he turned and said, "Looks like I'll have to figure out how to get myself owl bit more often."

"Be sure and use cold water," I said.

***

I drove past my turn at the river and stayed north on the highway into town. My shift was only four hours, so I still had time to go into Bend and pick up a loaf of Great Harvest bread. Howard would grumble about the birdseed in it, and I'd explain to Howard, yet again, that millet is a grain, and it's good for you.

Truth be told, the bread was an excuse to delay going home. I'd seen those two naked, but I was the one exposed. I was the one on the wrong side of the glass.

I parked down the block from the bakery, but never made it past the clearance rack in front of Luci's Luscious Boutique. Luci was having an end of season sidewalk sale. Half price on all summer dresses and sarongs. That's what the naked woman was wearing, a sarong. I ran my hand along the many colors of soft fabric. Picked up one that reminded me of the river, full of swirls and ripples and deep pools of color.

"That's a great color for you," said a girl squeaking hangers along the rack next to me. She wore a leather mini skirt with a halter top and a nose ring. "It'd go perfect with the silver in your hair," she said.

"Oh, I could never wear this," I said. "But the fabric is pretty, isn't it? Just to have around, maybe to cover a window?" I unfolded the cloth and held it out.

"Why wouldn't you wear it?" The girl looked me up and down, from my fitted snap button shirt to my jeans. "You've got a good shape. And besides, anyone can wear a sarong. My boyfriend wears one. They're sexy."

***

On my way out of town I passed Jack going the opposite way in his pickup. He had some woman in the truck with him. All I could tell was that she had dark glasses and long dark hair, some of it blowing streamers out the open window. I lifted my arm to wave, but my hand never made it past the steering wheel.

Jack didn't see me anyway.

***

At home I stood naked in front of my mirror. The girl with the nose ring was right. Even at seventy I still have a shape. I draped the soft fabric of the sarong around my bare skin. The sarong came with a brochure full of line drawings and written instructions for different ways to wear it. The over-the-shoulder style was the most flattering. It was an awkward reach, but I managed to tie the knot myself.

I wore the sarong into the living room. But for having exchanged his burgundy bathrobe for gray sweats, Howard was sitting exactly as I'd left him that morning.

"Look, Howard," I said. "See what I found on sale?"

Howard muted the TV and watched while I turned, first one way, then the other, like a fashion model at the end of a runway.

"Where's the toga party?" Howard said, sunken beyond comfort into the sofa.

"It's a *sarong*," I said.

"What for?" Howard said. He aimed the remote and changed channels. He looked up at me still standing there and said, "Come here, Babycakes," He patted the seat beside him. I sat down. My body fell into his, so deep was the depression he made on the sofa. The volume on the TV was too loud, gunshots and breaking glass, a car crashing through a department store window.

"You don't like it?" I said. I lifted the fabric of the sarong.

Howard patted my thigh the way you'd pat an old dog. "It's not you, Ellie," he said.

I got up and faced Howard. "You don't even know me," I said. I stood right in front of the TV. He gave me a confused look, his eyes like what you see in a nursing home.

I saw past Howard, across the river to where there was nothing but nature and a searing September sunset coming through the branches of the broken-top ponderosa. The way the window was lit, you could see every streak and smudge. So much naked glass for a woman my age. Impossible to keep clean. We needed curtains.

"You're standing right in front of the TV," Howard said. "I can't see a thing."

I went back to my room and tugged at the knot over my left shoulder. The fringe at the edge of the fabric was snarled into the knot and it wouldn't come loose. My neck was sore from trying to see how to get it undone. I got my sewing scissors and cut through the knot.

Cosmo

Cosmo was the guy who pulled over in a faded VW van after my '56 Chevy ran out of gas between Abilene and Sweetwater. They were having a gas war along that stretch of highway, and I was holding out for under twenty cents a gallon. This was 1971, a time when such things were still possible. Anything was possible so long as you got out of Texas, away from Dallas, where the threat of all eternity in hell was the glue that kept your parents from divorce, and Bill Bradley's idea of a date was spinning out the rear tires of his red Mustang on roadkill to see how high he could flip a dead cat. Not even a movie, and you're supposed to let him take you parking? You're supposed to get in the back seat?

I wanted completely out of Texas.

Cosmo had crazy hair, a full dark beard, and eyes like St. Francis. But most of all, Cosmo had California license plates. I grabbed my things and left the Chevy for dead.

***

One of Cosmo's invisible guides told him to take me to a certain canyon in Northern Arizona. A place you had to drive through bare bones desert to find, miles and miles of dirt road, until you came to a handful of beat vehicles parked at an edge where the earth dropped off. Down below was a river lined with plush pockets of green. A steep scramble from the rim, and we were on a path through sycamore and cottonwood trees, prickly pear and mesquite, rocks and sand. And a sweet balm in the air, a fragrance as hard to catch as butterflies.

About a mile or so into the canyon, we heard mysterious music. Something flutey that drifted in and out. A few more twists in the river and the canyon narrowed. We climbed up the narrow along its right edge, around a deep bend, and then we were above the source of the music. We looked down on a deep pool of green water. A group of naked men and women were out like starfish on a slab of rock below. On the other side of the pool, a naked guy with long braids pulled himself up a sunburnt cliff, fingers and toes.

We worked our way down. Naked people smiled at us as if they weren't naked. Across the water, the cliff guy came down through the air head first. He vanished into the pool. I stood there and held my breath, watching for him to surface. On the water a mirrored orange canyon wall reassembled its fractured face. No one else seemed worried about the vanished cliff diver. Long breathy modulations floated high and low, echoed from faraway, so you thought there was another and another and another flute.

Cosmo was busy trying not to tip over while he took off his pants. The cliff diver surfaced and pulled himself back up the cliff, fingers and toes.

The flute player was on a ledge, a bit above the rest of us. She was how I wanted to be. I decided then and there to stop shaving my armpits. She sat perfectly naked with her legs crossed and her back straight, her head turned to the side, fingers smooth and elegant on a wood flute, eyes closed like the Blessed Virgin Mary on a holy card. She had her lips to the hollow wood, but the whole canyon was her instrument.

I took off all my clothes too. I undressed naked before the eyes of strangers and pretended this was normal.

***

They lived in caves along the river. Geronimo himself, they said, hid from the army in one of the caves. Now these people were make believe Apaches. Like I said, this was 1971, a time when such things were still possible.

All the good caves close to the water were taken, so Cosmo and I moved into a cave at the end of a dry side canyon. Nothing but rocks. No water, no sound of water, only the complicated song of a canyon wren. You had to climb up about ten or twelve feet to get to the cave, but after you'd done it a few times you knew where to put your fingers and toes.

As far as I knew, no one ever came along the jumble of boulders that led to our cave. Or if they did make it far enough to look up at its dark mouth, they probably turned back when they heard what we were doing. What we were doing, according to Cosmo, was healing our second chakras.

Cosmo didn't want me to call it fucking, but after twelve years at Saint Monica's Girls School you can't help but talk like that once in awhile. I told Cosmo once how good he was at fucking, and his eyes went limp, along with everything else, until whatever it was had passed through him like gas pains. Then he was back with me, his scraggly-haired face over mine, his St. Francis eyes tame and wild at the same time. The deeper Cosmo loved me, the more I blubbered for fear he'd leave.

There's nothing to make you so worried as being loved like that.

***

Our cave was behind where there had once been a waterfall. The cave had been carved by water or humans, probably a combination of both. We had a convenient smokehole near the entrance. Above the cave the old watercourse smoothed into a dry wash, clotted with dark runty juniper. You could drop dead juniper wood down the hole directly into the fire pit at the entrance.

The cave had a front room where we did all our living, a middle room that was too dark for anything but storing our backpacks, and a tunnel you had to crawl through on your belly while you tried to not think about flash floods. You tried especially hard to not think about tarantulas or snakes. You wormed your way along an uphill grade through cool invisible sand until you were in a darkness so black your eyes would never adjust. And if you went against all instinct and pushed onward to the end of the tunnel, you ended up in a domed chamber big enough for a dozen or more people. The Inner Chamber.

I only went back there once, and I got out as soon as I'd lit a candle and searched for anything that could come out and bother us in our sleep, anything moving or dead.

Cosmo, on the other hand, went back there on a regular basis.

Cosmo crawled into the Inner Chamber to meet with his invisible guides.

***

They told him to stop talking. He said he didn't know for how long, then not another word. At first I went along with it, his St. Francis eyes said enough. And in the dark of the night I'd answer to his body. I answered as wild and true as those silver fish in the canyon when they'd shoot out of the water to strike at the moon.

But I couldn't let it be.

"Why won't you talk to me, Cosmo?" I said. We were on our backs alongside the mouth of the cave, between our zip-together sleeping bags, waiting for the sun. Cosmo, the one closest to the edge, was watching the ragged patch of sky you could see from inside the cave. He said nothing.

"You think I should stop talking too? Is that what you're saying?" I propped myself up on one elbow, tried to insert myself between Cosmo and whatever was so interesting outside. It was a faraway hawk, lit up from underneath. Red tail. I dropped back to my side of the bed and curled in on myself, my back to Cosmo, hawk, sunrise.

"Tell me you aren't trying to fuck with my head," I said.

***

One hot day the sun stalled in the middle of the sky. A bunch of us were at one of the river's few sandy beaches when someone showed up with a watermelon so big it filled his backpack. A gift for the tribe, he said. Afterwards, I went in the waist deep water with an older guy named River Dancer. River Dancer had a gray ponytail, but his face was shaved smooth, and his chest was twice as built as Cosmo's. He splashed water on my front, then wiped watermelon juice and sticky sand from my cheek, my chin, my breasts. His hands were touching certain places too soon for me to know how I felt, but his alpha eyes dared me to act like this was normal.

Cosmo was in the middle of a seed spitting contest. He stood on the beach, a stick in one hand, a piece of watermelon in the other. He drew a line in the sand and

Laurel declared him the winner.

Back in our cave, watching the evening go purple, I said to Cosmo, "Is it because of River Dancer? Is that why you still won't talk to me?"

Silence but for the scrabble of the ringtail who lived in a hole beneath us.

"Tell me you're not burnt out on me," I said. "Tell me you wouldn't rather be with Laurel." Laurel of the celestial flute. Laurel in whose presence I always said or did something clumsy. Laurel, the Goddess of Cool.

"You're just trying to make yourself dark and mysterious to attract women, aren't you?" I couldn't shut up. "How long will it be before your guides tell you to worship at the altar of *Laurel's* body?"

Like drowning in quicksand. The more you thrash, the deeper you get sucked in.

"You're mad at me," I said.

"You're trying to punish me for something," I said.

"You're abandoning me," I said.

Cosmo sat there under starlight and stone, and his head went back and forth—no, no, no—after each thing I said. Down canyon an owl hooted.

And even though I didn't believe all the things I was saying, once I said them, I had to act as if I did. I unzipped our zip-together sleeping bags. I made our bed two separate things.

Cosmo watched with his St. Francis eyes. He didn't say a word.

***

Then one day he did. For no reason at all, other than his guides said it was time to start talking again. I was gathering water jugs and dirty dishes to take to the river, when Cosmo crawled out from the tunnel after a night in the Inner Chamber. He stood on the edge and looked down at the seared boulders below.

"You ready for a swim?" he said. Like the last couple of weeks had never happened. Like I hadn't gone off on a supply run with River Dancer and stayed gone until way past noon the next day. Like nothing in the world mattered but crossing those hot rocks to the green river below.

We left our washed dishes under the sycamore tree near the entrance to our canyon and hiked upstream toward the source of the river. Springs gushed from cracks in the dry earth. Beyond this spot the main canyon widened into juniper desert, but here was where the green things started. The shrubs and grasses and cottonwood and sycamore trees. And that certain something that drifted the air with its smell so sweet you'd spend the rest of your life sniffing the wind.

We filled our jugs, then went down to the first good pool. I swam under Cosmo's legs, stood on my head underwater, scissor-kicked the sky. Cosmo floated me on my back, his head blocking the sun. His hair was twisted black snakes, haloed in silver light. Inside the halo his face was dark and biblical.

Later, when we were on our backs in the sand, I asked Cosmo, "What if your guides told you to fuck Laurel?"

"My guides would never tell me to *fuck* anyone," Cosmo said.

"You know what I mean," I said.

A grasshopper clattered. It's a sound that, until you know better, goes off like a rattlesnake. I rolled over to my belly and propped up on my elbows. I kept an eye on the edge of the dry grass.

"The only reason you're with me is because your guides

said so," I said. "What's to stop your guides from telling you you'd be better off with someone else?"

"Well, they wouldn't unless that was the right thing to do." Cosmo put his forearm over his eyes. His armpit had dark hair and the only white skin on his body. I wanted to burrow my face in there.

"What's to stop your guides from lying?" I said. "What if you're delusional?"

That night I zipped together our zip-together sleeping bags. I'd been with River Dancer, but only once, and only to get back something I thought Cosmo had taken from me. I even had it worked out, what I'd say if Cosmo ever asked me about that night. I'd tell him that *my* guides told me to fuck River Dancer.

***

Cosmo's invisible guides told him to stop eating the food we'd carried in on our backs. After a few days of nothing but the watercress we found in the burbling springs downriver, his breath smelled like something a dog would roll around in. And he was already too skinny.

Then Cosmo stopped wearing clothes altogether. He found an old blanket that a long ago flood had left tangled in the thorny branches of some shrubs. It was dirt colored and pressed into solid brittle folds when he pulled it free, but turned out to be faded pink once it was rinsed in the river. Cosmo carried the blanket with him everywhere. Dark skinned and emaciated, he could have been a model for *National Geographic*.

Along with his blanket, he started carrying a crooked stick with a fork lashed to one end. He used it as a walking staff, fork end up. Or he'd squat on a rock in the river like someone who'd never known furniture, his eyes fixated on the water, his fork poised like a spear.

You'd see him on his back in the sand, waving his arms and legs. And you'd want to go cover his nakedness. You'd want to take his faded pink blanket and at least cover his cock with it. You'd close your eyes, but you could still hear him laughing, or whatever those sounds were. You might think of hyenas. You might think of crows. You might see Nurse Ratched holding out a straight jacket.

And when all you could hear were the loose sounds of mourning doves and water, you'd open your eyes, and there would be nothing but the imprint his body had left in the sand.

***

On the evening of the full moon I made what had used to be Cosmo's favorite supper. Barbecued beans and creamstyle corn, the two cans mixed together in one pot, you don't even have to heat it. He lay wasted on our zip-together sleeping bags and wouldn't eat any. I took it out on the ledge near the mouth of our cave and ate the whole pot myself.

Cosmo crawled off, dragging his blanket, into the Inner Chamber.

Someone had given me a few dried peyote buttons for the full moon. Hard dirt colored clods. I used the tip of my Swiss army knife to clean out the warty bumps on top. The warts released a white fluff that was supposedly strychnine. I made a small fire and brewed some of the buttons in a tea. It tasted so nasty I vomited.

The last supper.

Barbecued beans and creamstyle corn. I knelt on the edge and watched corn ooze down the rock. Next I tried to swallow broken bits of peyote like pills. I managed to get a few rough dry pieces down with spoonfuls of peanut butter.

Dusk turned into night. The moon came up over the east rim. I left the cave and headed down in the moonlight toward the river. The rock was warm and friendly under my naked feet, and my feet knew each boulder and stone by its fit. My feet knew what the rocks knew, remembered how it feels to be shaped by water. I made it to within sight of the sycamore tree that lived at the junction to our canyon. She stood alone and rippled her smooth white arms like a belly dancer.

Everything. Everything under the moon was alive and moving in the perfect way for what that thing was. All I could do was drop to my knees and weep for all the times I walked right by and missed it.

You'd think it would make a difference. You'd think that once you'd caught God in the act you'd wake up more holy.

I woke up naked and sweating on top of our zip-together sleeping bags with the sun hot and high, licking the edge of our bed. Cosmo was crouched by my feet and trembling faster than a rattler's tail. He looked so buzzed that I pulled back when he reached to touch my hand.

I sat up and put on my cutoffs and yellow T-shirt. Cosmo's eyes were just too much. "What is going on with you?" I said.

"White light," Cosmo said. "You don't see it?"

I looked outside and the rocks were bright enough to hurt your eyes, but that's how it got around this time of day, especially from inside the cave.

Cosmo's eyes were all pupil, explosive wet black.

It turned out that Cosmo was blind. Or rather the opposite of blind. Instead of darkness, Cosmo saw only light. He had to feel his way around the cave with his hands. He bumped into rock. He couldn't find the water jug. He saw me though. Or rather my shape. He said I was made of light. I moved my hand in front of his face, and he could follow its motion. I asked him what he saw. "Diamonds," he said. "Diamonds streaking with light."

I put the water jug in Cosmo's hands and he drank. He needed to cut his fingernails. They were cracked and dirty.

***

I worked my way down the river, calling up into caves, trying to find anyone. Most of them had moved north to places like Oregon and Colorado. It was godforsaken hot. I had to go all the way to the bend with the deep green pool before I found the few who were left. I told them what was happening to Cosmo.

"I think he's delirious," I said. "I was afraid to leave him alone."

A man named Ahimsa said, "He's got his sixth chakra wide open. That can be dangerous. Like walking around without your skin on."

I nodded my head like Laurel and the others were doing, as if I had a *clue* what they were talking about. "And he hasn't eaten anything in over two weeks," I said. "Do you think maybe…?" I looked at their faces, hoping someone else would say the rest. No one did. "Maybe he should, I don't know, see a doctor?"

***

I couldn't get Cosmo's van to start, so River Dancer drove us to Flagstaff in his house truck. I didn't know what to give them for his last name when we half-carried, half-dragged Cosmo into the emergency room. They said it would take some time. They said they didn't know how long. They said they needed to admit him into the hospital for observation.

They said there were several possibilities.

Cosmo said nothing and I dared not look into his St. Francis eyes.

River Dancer was headed for Colorado. He said Colorado would be cool after Arizona. He said he'd take me with him, if I wanted to come. He drove me back to the canyon and waited for me on the rim while I hiked the miles back down to the cave. I grabbed my things and made it back to the rim by sunset.

We left Cosmo's van for dead.

***

I woke up the next morning to roosters and a distant baby crying. I was still in my cutoffs and yellow T-shirt on top of River Dancer's bed in his house truck. We'd driven late into the night and landed at someone's place near Sedona, but I'd been too wasted to go inside and say hi to whoever lived there.

Now I got up and walked through a dirt yard scattered with toy parts and tricycles, past a faded blue school bus with broken windows and into an old adobe house. Inside was cool and dark.

A woman with her hair in two long braids stood in the kitchen with a baby on her hip. She turned from the stove and asked if I'd like some tea. She said her name was Dawn, and the baby was Sundance. Her two older kids were still in bed sleeping. So was River Dancer.

"He'll probably be crashed out till noon," she laughed. "You know how he is."

I made myself sit there and drink peppermint tea until Dawn went to change the baby's diaper. Then I snuck out before I'd have to meet any more of River Dancer's kids or girlfriends or wives.

I hitched back to Texas and settled for Bill Bradley and

his red Mustang.

***

I called the Flagstaff hospital from Dallas. This was two divorces later, around the mid-eighties. I was hoping something might still be possible. But without ever knowing his last name, that far back? Forget it. Then the woman on the other end lowered her voice and said, "Honey, are you hunting some man who left you with a baby?"

"No," I said.

I'd never had any babies, but that was none of her business.

She went on in her secretive voice, "Because I happen to know for a fact that the state will get involved if it's a deadbeat dad."

"Cosmo would never abandon anyone," I said. I hung up the phone.

***

My search engine tells me there are 597,000 matches for Cosmo. In only the first dozen or so you come up with a Cosmo who raises red worms, Cosmo's cult movie site, Cosmo the tango master.

I tell myself it doesn't matter. I tell myself that the one man who didn't piss on my heart could just as easily be some scraggly old bum lost in conversation with himself. Waving his hands in front of his face to make some point. Dirty hands with broken yellow fingernails. One of those men you cross the street to avoid.

I tell myself to forget Cosmo, the whole idea is impossible.

***

I keep having this dream. In the dream there's a fake old west ghost town on the rim of our canyon. Behind the false store fronts, it's a tourist trap shopping mall. There are no other people in this dream, no clerks, no customers. I'm alone, wedged between racks of tourist t-shirts, or crammed against a glass counter full of Indian jewelry. I'm spinning the earring display, turquoise, silver, bear paw imprints, wolves howling at the moon. Not what I want, where is the canyon? I make my way through the clutter, enter a long empty corridor, weathered wood creaking under my feet. I follow it to the end of the mall, open a small door and here is a flight of rickety wooden stairs. I go down the stairs, zigzagging a cliff face down into the canyon. Nothing is as it should be, the river bank is a mowed chem-lawn with picnic tables on slabs of cement. The river runs through a concrete channel, flat and straight between concrete spillways.

"I've had this dream before." This is what I say to myself in the dream. In the dream I remind myself that I've had this dream again and again and again. Only *this* time, I tell myself, *this* time it's not a dream. And I try to find my way back to the cave, but nothing is as it should be, and I grow weary, I give up. And now come the tears, the sobbing and shaking. In the dream I don't even try to hold myself together. In the dream I just fall apart. I weep a pure grief like nothing I've ever known in real life. Until I wake up in my bed with dry eyes and thank God that it's only a dream.

This happens every few months, year after year after year. Different details, but always the same dream. And I never find my way back to our cave.

The thing that gets to me about this dream is how it keeps tricking me into believing that it's real.

ANOTHER SUNRISE

I landed upside down, my mouth full of Fig Newton. How peculiar, that I remembered the name of this sweet paste in my mouth. Newton, what an odd name for a cookie. My teeth were grinding fig seeds and this meant I was still alive. I wasn't sure if being alive was a good thing or just one more example of things gone wrong.

I opened my eyes then, opened my eyes to drifting dust and luminous streaks of pink and orange and gold. The same sunrise that had been flaunting itself in my rearview mirror, just daring me to take my eyes off it. And then the dark shape of a cow standing broadside in my headlights, its head turned my way, stupid eyes unblinking, my foot mashing the brake, hands fighting the wheel. Blinding dust and the sound of gravel hitting metal like gunshot. A terrible lifting and turning.

And now this ticking stillness, this Fig Newton still in my mouth. I wondered if I could swallow upside down or should I just leave things alone awhile longer, or maybe spit it out. No, it would fall up my nose. And I saw how strange this all was, that I should continue to dwell on the Fig

Newton. I saw what I was doing, how I was using what was in my mouth to avoid a certain reckoning. So I swallowed, and it was surprisingly easy.

It didn't even occur to me until it happened, that if you unbuckle your seatbelt when you're hung like that, you'll drop like a corpse. I crawled out the open window and collapsed, my heartbeat pounding the earth. I rolled over and rubbed my neck, felt my face with both hands, then my skull and was startled by the texture of my fresh buzz cut. I touched myself under my shirt. My ribs were whole, nothing seemed to be leaking. I still had both breasts, they were still soft and warm, and I lay there on my back and held them as if for the last time.

Then I worked myself up on all fours, turned my neck this way and that. I looked around for the cow, dead or alive. Nothing. I rose on knees that were weak and shaking. Decided they too had escaped injury, not that it mattered whether or not my knees were still fit for Swan Lake.

I knelt in that roadside ditch, my arms, my face lifted to the sky, and I cried out, "Thank you, Jesus!" And then I yelled, "Did you hear that, Jean Marie? Are you happy now" As if either of those two had an ear for sarcasm.

***

By the time the sun came up over the eastern mountains I was on my way. I had on decent hiking shoes, but other than that I wore only shorts and a sleeveless blouse and Jean Marie's green baseball cap. I walked fast against the early morning chill, then faster out of respect for the rising power of the sun. I was headed deeper into the wild country and not back toward the pavement. I held steady to the destination that had pulled me through the night. It couldn't be that much farther, although you'd never suspect, from looking across this landscape, that there was a river nearby. A river scratching its way through millions of years of stone.

Up here on the high plateau, sagebrush cast long low shadows across the road. Cow plops were strung along one side and the hoof marks of antelope made sharp crossings in the dust. I turned back and there were my footsteps down the middle of this powdery road, their oddly ornate tread pattern. And off in the distance, Jean Marie's Pathfinder, on its back like some kind of dead insect. Lit by sunrise, it was as golden as a chrysalis.

***

I heard the sound of an engine, the rattling approach as someone drove up behind me. I moved to the left side of the road, but did not change my pace, did not turn around to look. I kept walking as if I were back in the city, as if I knew where I was and knew where I was going. As if I hadn't a care under the sun about who a woman might meet out here.

A dirty white pickup rolled past, something lashed to the hood. I glimpsed a dark face in an open window, a small camper shell under a roof rack loaded with tipi poles. Their tips swayed up and down as the truck bounced over a pothole and came to a stop ahead of me. I had no choice but to walk up alongside.

"Need a lift?" said the driver.

I stopped. I turned my head and looked. He had long dark hair traced with silver. A face right off the reservation, a face watching mine. I looked away. I saw smears of blood on the hood, spiraled twists of rope over tawny fur, the dark pads of a large paw, the tips of its claws. I stood there sweating under Jean Marie's baseball cap. The dust from his tires hung heavy in the air. I pulled down the brim of the cap, gazed off to the south and wondered if I'd taken a wrong turn in the night.

"How far is Two Forks?" I said.

He turned off the engine and bent to look up through the windshield. A buzzard drifted up there and nothing else, not a trace of cloud left. This far along and the sky had lost everything.

"Further than you want," he said in a quiet voice.

He got out, this big barefoot Indian wearing nothing but Tweety-bird pajama pants. I stepped back into the brush until it poked my bare legs. He walked around the front of his truck and opened the passenger door. The sound of clanking metal. Crowbars, axes, guns—I couldn't see what all he was moving from the passenger seat to the floor. Then he went to the back and opened the hatch and tailgate, rummaged around back there, and slammed things shut. A puff of dust rose in the air. He came closer, still empty-handed. He now wore a pair of flip-flops that slapped his feet at every step. He lifted a dust-covered foot to step back into the truck, but then he stopped and he turned to me. It was hard not to stare at his fat brown belly, its skin as smooth as a woman.

"Come on," he said. He pointed to the passenger side.

I tried to blink the dust out of my eyes. Squinted toward the wavering south. I was looking for the shape of a lone juniper tree that marked the spot where the road would drop out of sight into the canyon, where I had intended to drop even deeper in Jean Marie's Pathfinder. Just then something bit the back of my knee. I whirled around and swatted myself, saw that the heel of my shoe was on the edge of a living anthill, I stepped back into the road and stomped my foot, brushed the little crawlers off my sock and leg. I looked at him then, his dark eyes were simply watching mine. He was waiting.

"Why not," I said. I walked around the front of the truck, the carcass on the hood. I got in where he'd made room for me and slammed shut the door. My feet were pressed against a metal tool box, and despite the heat, I wished for long pants to cover my legs. But he wasn't looking at my legs or anything else, he sat there with one hand on the key in the ignition and he seemed to be staring at nothing on the road before us.

"Here's the deal," he said, and he leaned toward the windshield and tipped his head to look up, and now there were three buzzards circling high. Buzzards up there, a batch of flies crawling over the filthy dashboard, this half-naked Indian.

"What?" I said, one hand on the door handle, prepared to jump and run.

"I don't want things to get weird between us," he said. He looked over at me and I saw his eyes were looking at my face and not lower down, but still I kept hold of the door handle.

"So I'm just asking you up front to keep your Jesus to yourself," he said. Then he started the engine and we drove off. I let go of the door handle and I leaned my head back on the seat.

"No problem," I said. I closed my eyes and felt the air blow in, cool and free across my face.

***

The rattling of my bones woke me up. That and the sound of my snoring. I jerked my head upright. My neck was sore, my mouth parched. I looked around for water, didn't see that he had any. My thighs were sticky where they touched the seat. I peeled them off, one at a time, then sat up straight and took hold of the handgrip above the window. We were lurching down the grade into the canyon over ruts and washouts and bulging boulders.

"Nice nap?" said the Indian, still keeping his eyes on the road.

"I wasn't asleep," I said. I held on and looked hard out my window, even though there was nothing but rocky slope and dead-looking scrub out there, the view down into the canyon was on his side. I saw the muscles of my arm, how hard I was clenching the handgrip, the blue veins inside my elbow. My breasts bounced freely inside my blouse and I felt my nipples touching loose cotton. And a black fear oozed through my chest.

I turned to the Indian. He was straining his neck to see over the thing on the hood. It was headless. A long tail, thick as my wrist, was bouncing around like something alive.

"That's a mountain lion," I said.

He said nothing, steered the truck around the first deadman's curve. His breasts were more jiggly than mine.

"Male or female?" I said.

"Female."

"Why'd you kill her?"

"I didn't," he said.

And now the canyon was on my side and I looked down, down, down to where I caught a glimpse of the river, a green radiance slicing through all that rock. I wondered if drinking from there would make me sick. I wondered if I cared.

At the next switchback the Indian pulled off the road. I laughed out loud that he should stop here, on this particular peninsula, this point that I'd been driving toward since the moment I peeled rubber in front of Jean Marie's house.

He turned at the sound of my laughter, then shrugged his shoulders and got out. Of course it wasn't really so odd, this was the obvious place to stop for the view. Or hold your wheel steady to the end.

I heard him open the rear of his camper, then he was back with two sweating bottles filled with something red and murky. "This'll do you," he said. He reached in across the seat and handed me a bottle. Then, leaving his door hanging open, he walked away.

I turned the glass bottle, there was no label, but what was inside was wet and cold, so I tried a sip. It had the earthy taste of mushrooms, or maybe roots, mingled with a tart fruity flavor, possibly some type of berry. I closed my eyes and I drank it down to the sediment at the bottom. Whatever kind of juice or tea or poisonous brew this might be, it was all I had against my thirst and my hunger and my not knowing what would happen next.

A drop of sweat crawled from my armpit, like a wet bug down to my waist. The sun came in through the open window, hot on my arm, hot on the side of my face. I pressed the cool bottle to my cheek, rolled it back and forth until the glass was as warm as my skin. I lifted the door latch and I got out. I felt myself touching the earth through the soles of my shoes and I felt my mind floating free of my head. The light was pulsing. My eyes were filled with the brilliant otherness of this land and, still holding the bottle by its neck, I slowly began to walk toward the edge of the canyon.

The Indian turned and watched my feet, my feet moving me closer to where he stood. I looked down then, and I saw how the ground was alive with loose shale, how my feet made a ringing music of each step. This was something new. I stopped and dug the toe of my shoe under a pile of flat stones, kicked them into the air just to hear the sound of their falling. From beneath the clatter there erupted a rattling buzz. In one motion I leaped backwards and threw my bottle at the noise. I was in the air as the glass shattered. My jump was a levitation that amazed me even as it was happening.

"Jesus fucking Christ!" I yelled. Both my feet were back on the ground, a record distance from where I'd been. I pressed my hands against the beating of my heart. The Indian had his head thrown back, he was just laughing, laughing, laughing.

"Well, so much for the silent Redman routine," I said. My eyes raked the ground back and forth, searching for what was underneath. The snake stayed hidden in its hole. I toe-stepped around the buzzing to where the Indian stood, silent again, his belly still shaking with laughter. I watched the spot until it was silent again, then reached out my arm for the bottle the Indian held in his hand. "Shut up and give me a hit of your medicine," I said. "I seem to have lost mine."

He handed it over and I drank what was left of the sludge at the bottom. "You got the legs of an antelope and a throwing arm like Sandy Koufax," he said. "And a mouth like no Born-Again I ever met."

"That happens to be my girlfriend's truck back there, *her* bumper stickers, *her* Jesus, not mine," I said, and was immediately annoyed with myself for giving him this useless information. I handed him back his empty drink.

"Whatever you say, Lefty." He looked me up and down, and I saw in his eyes the kind of measuring I used to get from a new ballet partner, before we'd begin our first dance.

I turned away from him then, turned my attention to the emptiness before me, then down to the green temptation of the river below. The river swirled around a bend and became lost in a mosaic of color and shadow and stone. A step closer and I felt myself held only by the weight of my bones. What a small motion it would take to tip over and fly freely into all that depth. Yes, it would be a cleaner way, boundless and more elegant to enter without a vehicle.

I moved on the edge until my toes were over empty air, then waited for what would happen. Waited to see if I would free myself from feeling.

I stood there and I felt the air of this place enter my lungs. The fragrance of sage, the ancient smell of stone, the scent of my sweat and the sweat of the Indian. He too had moved closer to the edge. I looked at him sideways, the smooth brown skin of his belly, his dark nipple, his man-breast. And I saw him now as I saw the river, as a shimmering aliveness at the center of this silent slow landscape. He turned his eyes to mine and we met each other for the first time in our eyes. And Indian or not, something essential was reconciled between us.

He reared on one leg and threw his bottle far over the abyss.

***

My shorts and shirt were in a pile by the water, all I had on was Jean Marie's baseball cap. I sat in the river facing the current and I drank freely from the water jug Artemus had placed on the rock beside me. The naked feel of the river, its gentle pull, its slow gurgle, I sat with my arms crossed over my spread apart knees and I peed whenever I got the urge. I let it all run through me.

Every now and then I turned my head to watch Artemus. He worked with a knife at a portable blue table. His Tweety-bird pajama pants were rolled above his knees and his hair was tied in a topknot.

What was left of the mountain lion, a headless skinned carcass, hung from a tripod of tipi poles. The rest of the poles were leaned into the crotch of the tripod to form a wickiup, open-sided to the north. The wickiup was covered with scraps of blanket and cloth, the only decent shade in this part of the canyon. Juniper trees grew on the hill, but down here was nothing but rock and sand and willow brush.

Back when I was here with Jean Marie, this river was too fast, too cold to sit here like this. The near side was pure snowmelt from the East Fork. You had to swim halfway across to get to the warmer current that flowed from the West Fork. A few miles up the West Fork was a place where hot springs gushed from the earth like God's answer.

It was spring then, but we still needed shade in the afternoon. We did like the animals, we stayed low under the narrow leaves of willow. Right where Artemus had parked his truck, driving over what had been our daybed, mine and Jean Marie's.

Last spring we were both pale after a winter in the city. Especially Jean Marie, with her copper hair and alabaster skin. She was as luscious as twice-risen bread dough. I knelt over her, one knee outside each of her thighs, and I looked down at her breasts and her belly and I called her beautiful, but she shook her head no. She said she was obese, and I put a finger over her mouth and said that was an ugly word and don't exaggerate. She turned her face to the side, she squeezed shut her eyes, not wanting to see me seeing her. I bent to rub sunscreen on her belly and her breasts. My hair dropped like a curtain from my shoulders. It was so long back then, free from its ballerina bun, trailing the contours of Jean Marie's flesh, while my fingers whispered the things she would not let in through her ears.

"Jean Marie," I said, my voice a ragged awakening back to the present, back to my body seated in the river, back to a future I didn't want. I tried to move my tongue inside my mouth, it was stuck. I lifted the plastic jug to my lips and drank more water, but no matter how much I drank my mouth was cotton. Some side effect from Artemus' brew.

I took off Jean Marie's baseball cap and ran my hand over the tips of my buzz cut, back and forth. I still couldn't believe this new texture against the palm of my hand, what it meant and that she would never know why I cut my hair. I glanced down, then closed my eyes against the sight of my breasts in the water. Opened them to look into Jean Marie's cap and there was the sweat stain from her forehead.

Jean Marie, who she was then.

A fish jumped, the same fat fish jumping up from the same spot as before where we said we'd bring our children here to fish, the children we planned to adopt, and Jean Marie agreed with me then. She said yes, yes this is some kind of holy and who needs church when you've got places like this.

***

I was wandering downstream, picking up driftwood for the fire. The sun was about to drop behind the rim and I turned to go back around the bend, to retrieve my clothes from the shore. But then a canyon wren started working the acoustics. This familiar piercing, this silvery song, how it startles with its cry, like the sudden discovery of loss. The descending, decelerating lament trailing off to a whimper of resignation. And then again, as sharp as an arrow hitting its mark. I stood in the cooling sand and I closed my eyes to listen. Four repetitions, then silence and my yearning for more.

Nothing beautiful ever lasts as long as you want.

I dropped my armload of wood, lifted a heel to the top of a waist-high boulder, hinged forward to stretch that leg, then did the other. I spread my arms and twirled. The canyon walls streaked across my sight, a blur of warm color. A few arabesques, my shadow long and naked on the sand. I danced my shadow to the base of a cliff and watched it leap like primitive art on a wall of stone. But my eyes were alert for the next rattlesnake and for Artemus, that he might come upon me dancing naked. I wasn't sure if I feared or wanted to be seen. I was a performer, I knew how I looked dancing, how I made motion appear effortless, that this was what I had worked for. This was what I had trained my body to do, to deliver on this one simple dream, to create the illusion that we humans can be free of our weight.

Yet I was not free of weight. I carried the weight of Jean Marie and the weight of her Pathfinder. The weight of the lumps in my breast. And how strange it was, that of all these things, what weighed most heavily in this moment was my nudity, the weight of having a man nearby.

But no, I would not stop. Man or no man, I would perform my dance. I would retrieve the canyon wren's song, I would feel things as honestly as if it were God and not some strange man who may or may not be watching.

***

A peach cobbler was leaking its juices from under the lid of a Dutch oven. The juice sizzled when it hit the coals, the smell of burnt sugar. And that other smell, juniper smoke, its scent more ancient than any temple incense, a fragrance to make you remember a life you might have had, a life from before you were born.

I sat on the ground with my chin on my knees, hugging

my legs inside Artemus' red sweatshirt. This oversize shirt and the hot coals were all I had to keep myself warm. I couldn't build up the fire, not until he said the cobbler was done. He was busy over a camp stove on his blue table, stirring up yet more smells, garlic and meat and fried onion. I was half-starved. I'd eat his mountain lion, no question.

Hunger and cold. These were feelings worth having.

This place got a lot colder at night than Boise. And I'd been in such a hurry to get away from Jean Marie, that I never even stopped for a jacket. Just jumped from the kitchen table and ran out the door and there was Jean Marie's hulking Pathfinder blocking my small Toyota. So I got down on my knees in the dark and felt around underneath until I found her magnetic key holder, and then, once I had the thing started and backed out of the driveway, I got a different idea. I peeled rubber and drove.

I drove out of the city, wind in my face. I drove west and then south and then west some more. My only stop was for gas and Fig Newtons at a crossroads called Last Chance. Then I left the pavement and I kept going into the emptiest space on the map. Driving through the black night, the upward tilt of the land was barely perceptible, until the air blew cold on my scalp. I put on a baseball cap that I found stuffed between the gearshift and the seat and I closed the window, then opened it again. I needed that cold rushing air against the heat of my rage at Jean Marie. How she'd been at the supper table, her eyes shut tight in prayer, her hands clasped, white-knuckled and hard above her plate, thanking her Lord Jesus for our health—I almost cut in and told her about *my* health, but held back to let her finish—thanking her Lord Jesus for her garden, for cucumbers and peppers and vine-ripe tomatoes. And then she went from vine-ripe tomatoes to Satan, and at first I thought she was talking about some pest in the garden, but no, it was me, she was asking Jesus to cast Satan out of my heart.

I told myself this wasn't Jean Marie, she'd been brainwashed. I reached across her plate and I grabbed her fist, still clenched in prayer, but she held her fingers locked tight inside my hand.

"Look at me," I said, rubbing the outside of her fingers with the insides of mine. "Have I ever done anything but love you?" My voice was pleading.

Her eyes were on my hand as if it had grown scales. She pulled her hands away and put them under the table, pressed her back into her chair. She wouldn't look at my face, only at my new haircut, the latest flaunting of my *depravity*.

I couldn't tell her then, about my visit to the clinic, how cutting off my hair was the only way I knew to take control over what was about to happen. All I could do was get out of her kitchen, out of her house, and if this was how she saw me, then out of her sight. I peeled rubber and then I got a different idea. All night I chased the headlight's beam. Until I caught sight of that sunrise. My last sunrise flaunting its depravity in the rearview mirror, the dark shape of a cow caught in the headlights, its head turned my way, stupid eyes unblinking.

"Earth to Lefty," said a man's voice. I looked up from the coals and was blinded by a beam of light from the center of Artemus' forehead, a headlamp. He handed me a loaded plate and a fork, then removed the Dutch oven and threw fresh wood on the fire. It smoldered, then came to life, lighting what was close, while the rest of the canyon was instantly lost in darkness.

Artemus sat on the ground across the fire and ate from the fry pan. Still half-naked, somehow staying warm in his skin, the tail end of his hair up like a feather from his topknot. I sat cross-legged, my knees poking out from under the sweatshirt, plate of food in my lap. I felt the emptiness in my stomach, the fire's heat on my knees. I poked the fork into a chunk of sauce-covered meat, but held back from taking that first bite. I watched Artemus eating from his pan.

"I've never been hungry like this," I said. "There's something that feels almost holy about being this hungry." I felt my face red from the fire, red from saying these things to an Indian who had given me his only plate and fork. His headlamp was turned off and it reflected dancing flames in the center of his forehead. His eyes were closed, his spoon poised empty in the air, jaw slowly moving. Artemus was alone with his food.

I sighed and shoved the fork in my mouth. Tasted the sauce, chewed the meat.

"This is really good," I said. "I mean *really* good."

"Cougar in rosemary sauce," said Artemus, "on a bed of wild rice."

"Who cooks like this on a camping trip?" I said.

"This isn't a camping trip," said Artemus.

I reached across the sand and poked my fork into the peach cobbler. Remembered my last Fig Newton and almost cried from being alive.

"It's the fresh nutmeg," said Artemus. He was deep into the Dutch oven with his spoon.

"You carry fresh nutmeg," I said. "But only one plate, one fork, one spoon."

"Less mess to clean up," he said.

Something whuffed off in the distance, a ghost or an owl

or some creature following its nose.

"Ever lonely?" I said.

"I go into town," said Artemus, "and before long they want to arrest me for some thing or other." He took off the headlamp and rubbed his forehead. "Those cops," he said, "they treat me like I'm some kind of drunk Indian."

"Are you?" I said.

"Yeah," he said.

"Well, I'm a dyke."

"I figured," he said.

"You're not drunk now," I said.

"Would be," he said, "if I had something to drink." He uncrossed his legs with a groan, stretched them out, then propped himself on his heels. "I need to get myself a new lawn chair," he said. "I busted through the old one." He scraped his spoon along the inside of the Dutch oven.

The light on his face was changing. I turned and looked over my shoulder and there was the moon. It was visibly pockmarked, past full with one side missing. The slightest scent of spoilage seemed to rise with the moon, some subtle shift in the breeze. I saw it now, what was left of the stripped carcass, lit by the moon and still hanging from the tripod. I turned back to the fire.

"That mountain lion," I said. "What happened to her head?"

"Getting stuffed," he said, his words muffled with cobbler.

"I got this nephew," Artemus said. "He threw it in a beer cooler and drove off into the sunrise. Thinks he can sell it and get rich."

"Your nephew killed her?" I said. "Like some kind of a *trophy* hunt?"

"More like a couple pickup loads of drunk Indians shooting at whatever shows up in the headlights."

"Well, I had a cow show up in my headlights," I said. "Jean Marie's headlights"

"She your girlfriend?" said Artemus.

"No," I said. "She's in love with Jesus."

"Every saint has a past, every sinner has a future," said Artemus.

"What the hell is that supposed to mean?" I said.

"Some upside down bumper sticker I read this morning."

"Oh, right," I said. "Jean Marie telling the world she's saved from being a lesbian." I poked a stick into the fire, which killed the flame and made it start smoking. Everything was smoked blue in the moonlight. Artemus got on all fours. Belly in the sand, butt in the air, he tipped his head sideways and with a slow steady breath, he blew the fire back into flame.

"My God is living," I said, "sorry about yours."

Artemus stood up and brushed his hands off on his Tweety-bird pajama pants. "I'm still breathing," he said.

"No, that's the bumper sticker on *my* car," I said, "which is probably what set off Jean Marie."

"That showed her," said Artemus. He wrinkled his nose and turned his face to the side. Where he stood, Artemus was a magnet for the smoke. He came around to my side of the fire.

"Listen," I said, "I came *this* close to putting my stupid bumper sticker on top of her stupid bumper sticker. I thought I showed a fair amount of restraint putting it on my car instead."

Artemus said nothing.

"What're you thinking?" I said.

"I'm thinking about fucking."

His leg was close enough I could have touched a Tweety-bird with my tongue. I tilted my face up toward his.

"Fucking *me*?" I said.

"I saw you dance," he said. "It brought things up for me."

"I thought I was alone," I said. "I used to be…" My words trailed into the fire, its dancing flames. "I'm a dancer," I said. "It's what I do. Besides, you were supposed to be back here messing with your lion."

"You're okay," he said. "I'm not gonna rape you. Even drunk, I don't do women that way."

"I know," I said and I drew my knees up, away from the fire.

And I did know. Ever since that morning on the rim when I'd stood there with my toes hanging over the edge and I'd felt him standing there beside me, and I knew he wouldn't try to stop me, knew he wouldn't reach out and grab me at the last moment. And I saw how this was a good thing, that he would leave me to decide on my own, that he would not impose himself.

The fire was down to coals again. The entire night was shades of blue under the moon.

"It's a genetic thing, right?" I said. "Indians and alcohol?"

"I've heard them say that," said Artemus.

"Breast cancer's like that," I said. "My mom, my aunt, my grandma."

Artemus stood quiet beside me.

"What about that stuff we drank on the way down?" I said.

"Medicine," said Artemus. "Helps me dry out. Helps me get right with myself."

"You got any more?"

His laugh was low and quiet. Bats swooped and fluttered like gigantic moths, their soft movement between us and the stars. Something brushed the top of my head. A batwing? A hand?

"Well?" I said. I nudged my head into his leg. Felt for a moment his thigh, through the flannel of his pants, his thigh touching my right temple.

"Tomorrow morning," he said, "before we go to the springs."

The hot springs. Reason enough for another sunrise. The springs and how it was for me there, my first and only time. The sound of water falling, falling, falling from one deep rock basin to the next and my body floating in the deep blue-green, my skin golden and rippled with wavelets of light. The canyon above and below me, rock and water and sky and the perfect solitude of the moment. Yet how I wanted Jean Marie to be with me. My disappointment when she wouldn't let me try to help her up the rocks to these pools, my sorrow when she just said she was too fat and out of shape and I should just go on without her. How badly I wanted her in that holy place with me.

"I wish we were there right now," I said. "I'd sleep warm in that water."

"You can sleep warm with me," said Artemus.

The firewood was all gone, the heat of the coals was fading, and I was nodding out against Artemus' leg. And his hand was on my head, touching my buzz cut. I rested my cheek on his thigh, into the soft flannel of his Tweety-bird pants and I dreamed of his belly, its skin as smooth as a woman.

Things Could Go Either Way

I will not wear animal skins in Seattle, no matter how much Benno talks and talks. Benno wants me to take off the real thing in my act. Arctic fox, wolf, seal. Benno wants me to end my show naked on the skin of a polar bear. "With a hunting knife between your teeth," says Benno.

Benno, he drives me to the airport and he talks. His words splash in one ear while my other ear listens to his tires slice the rain on the road. Benno says close the window before the rain ruins his interior. He hands me the white hanky from his breast pocket and tells me to wipe off the seat. The white hanky has *B* for Benno and *R* for Rudolph, written in white silky thread. The letters swoop and swirl, how a skater would dance them on ice.

Myself, I don't dance on ice, I dance on wood in a ground fog of cigarette smoke. All of us dancers know that Benno Rudolph is good for a ride to the airport. If you're traveling Greyhound, you're on your own. Benno Rudolph says bus stations attract the lowest class of perverts. Myself, I've never been on a Greyhound. Where I come from we use sled dogs and snow machines this time of year. Most of my people have never seen a bus. Or a hanky.

I wipe the hanky across leather the color of old blood. I keep my thoughts. My thoughts see the tip of my knife blade punch through Benno Rudolph's interior. And why not? There was no dignity in the death of the animals who gave these skins.

Benno, he talks and he talks. He says taking people to the airport is no fun anymore. He says he misses standing at the window and seeing the plane take off. What Benno really misses is watching his own reflection against the backdrop of planes taking off. The shape of his jacket, the line of his trousers against the night, the touch of his hanky to one eye.

We move through the wet lights of Seattle. Benno takes a fresh hanky from his cache between the seats. "This particular fold is called The Cagney," he says. "Notice how the two middle points are slightly off center." Benno, he talks and he talks. A leaky faucet that's been left running too long. Just last week we all had to sit around past closing while Benno talked and talked over a Tiramisu cake that said Happy Birthday Benno. The Tiramisu cake had the number 55 written in the same white swirl as the letters on his hanky. Lacy Davenport whispered in my ear that Benno must be fixated on fives, he has the same numbers on his cake every year.

Benno has me steer while he puts the hanky in his left breast pocket. He flips down the mirror, adjusts the points. "And remember," he says, his hands back on the wheel, "never allow the monogram to show above your pocket."

And now we're at the airport, at the passenger unloading zone next to the sign for Alaska Airlines. Benno, he must get out and stand with one hand on the hood of his silver

Mercedes. I grab my duffle from the back seat. Benno pokes a kiss on my cheek. He gives my ass a quick smack toward the door.

I whip around and hold the point of my knife to his belly.

Benno's eyes wake up. They go from the knife to my eyes. This man, I know what he needs. I know what it takes to wake him up. The knife holds us together in the moment.

"Not enough fat," I say. "You would insult my blade." The knife is no more than a factory featherlite, but I speak in this way for Benno, what he wants from a Native, what he expects a hunter would say. I snap the knife shut and drop it in with his hanky. The knife takes down two points of his four-point fold. "Hold on to that for me," I say.

"Only if you promise to bring us some furs," Benno says.

I rub the prickle of Benno's mustache off my cheek and go inside.

At the security gate a woman has me take off my boots, then a man slides his hand inside my duffle. The man moves his hand through my things while he smears a look all over my mouth. I lick my lips and head toward the pack of people at the entrance tunnel. Here is my last look into the wet night, out through the crack where the tunnel doesn't quite meet the plane. Down there men in yellow slickers are driving carts across streaks of red, green, and yellow reflected light. I fill my lungs with soggy air, then cross into the plane and turn the corner into first class.

First class aisle seat, there is a man with his head back, his throat laid open. The man's eyes are half-closed, probably blue or green or hazel, one of those colors that changes with the sky, with whatever he's wearing. He's wearing a gray-brown suit, the color is called taupe when it's a suit.

Benno has been teaching me suits.

The man in the taupe suit, his eyes are half-closed, but underneath he's waking up. He wakes up and watches me under half-closed lids.

All the people in first class are waking up and watching me down the aisle. They're trying to figure something out. It's my face. Too broad, too strong. It's my mouth. Too big. It's my hair. Like Benno said when he first found me working the street, "You can't have Godiva hair like that without men wanting to see you in it naked." Benno, he named me for my hair.

It brings laughter to my people at home, that a white man named me Raven.

I baby step my boots through first class, taking good care for the heels of the person in front of me. Getting everyone loaded into coach class is like squeezing toothpaste into a tube. Something I did earlier today, while Benno leaned in the doorway, elbow on his arm, arm across his chest, one finger tapping time on his dyed mustache. "For pity's sake, Raven," he said, "let's stop on the way to the airport and buy you a travel size Pepsodent!"

My people, we are not like that. It takes a steady hand and a calm mind to squeeze toothpaste from economy to travel size. I stayed where I was by the sink and I kept my thoughts. My thoughts saw Benno touching his white hanky to one eye as the sun slipped over the edge of the world to disappear for the next two months. My thoughts saw Benno sitting still by a hole in the ice for hours, maybe days, as long as it would take for something to stick its head out. I smiled and continued to squeeze Pepsodent. Steady hand, calm mind. For as long as it takes.

I can stand here in first class and watch the man in the

taupe suit for as long as it takes. Overhead bins snap open, slam shut. The man in the taupe suit, he looks at what I'm wearing and his face is not pleased.

I smile and I keep my thoughts. Benno, he was in my closet pawing through hangers and growling about us missing my plane. He took out the hanger with my red silk shirt and held it under his neck. He stroked the red silk down his chest. "You never know who you might meet on an airplane," he said. "Especially in the intimacy of a night flight." I said, "Why not?" to the red silk and "No," to the tight pants Benno held up next. "It's a fucking red-eye," I said, "I'm keeping things loose." Benno's face was not pleased. "Loose and easy-access," I said, then gave Benno my smile.

Benno would pick the man in the taupe suit. His look, Benno would say, his look is front line. That's what the suit says to the world. The suit says player, the suit says money, the suit says business all over. The man in the taupe suit is not yet in command, but he's front line. Notice how he sits, Benno would say. The man in the taupe suit sits fully reclined with his legs stretched out. He's average size, but he fully occupies his first class seat.

And now his careless white throat is near enough to slice with a thin blade knife. Near enough to reach down with my mouth and give it a kiss.

The man in the taupe suit closes his eyes against the many bodies pushing through to coach. He drops the curtain before I've warmed up my act. I shift my bag just enough to bump his knee. He grips the armrest. On his hand, a gold wedding band. He snaps open his eyes. See-through blue. His eyes are ice melting up and down my body.

I stop moving. Let the others pile dirty looks on my

back. Me and the man in the taupe suit, we're about to have a moment.

I turn to him, my face wide as the moon. Look at his mouth in a way that makes him look at mine. My mouth, my lips, my smile. I show him my strong clean teeth. Good teeth are reassuring to a white man. Benno says no first class white man will look at a native with rotten teeth, no matter how perfect the rest of the body. Benno says I am the first Eskimo with a set of teeth he would allow in his club.

Benno says I have a mouth that destroys marriages.

The man in the taupe suit watches my lips and I watch his. The skin around the lips of a white man, so soft and prickly at the same time.

His see-through eyes move slow as winter down the length of my hair, all the way down to my crotch. His eyes go baby-boy blue. And before I pass on into coach, I bend and bring my mouth to his ear. "Nice suit," I say, barely above a whisper. And this is not what the man in the taupe suit expects from an Eskimo wearing sandstone canvas Carhartts over a red silk shirt.

***

First on, first off, first class.

The man in the taupe suit is long gone when I pass through first class on my way out of the plane.

"Enjoy your stay in Anchorage," says the steward who fluffed my pillow. But I have no stay in Anchorage. Anchorage is as temporary as the moving hallway they roll between the airplane door and the terminal.

Outside, between the terminal and the small twin-engine that will take me home, I stop and look up. The night is hidden by floodlights, but nothing can hide this wind. The wind lifts and spreads my hair. The wind enters my flesh through the loose sides of my overalls, through the red silk shirt that Benno likes me to wear.

"Raven my love, you can dress like a carpenter on your own time," Benno said on the way to the airport, "but at the Erotic Exotic you're mine." I knew where Benno was going with this. "Forget it," I said. "It's fake fur or nothing." But Benno, he must talk and talk. "The Erotic Exotic is culture," he said. "The Erotic Exotic is art. For Christ's sake, your fake fur is the mustache on my Mona Lisa!" Talk and talk and talk. "You're not the only talented Eskimo on the planet, there's plenty more where you came from." Leaky faucet talk, until I reached across the car and grabbed Benno's chin with my hand and twisted it toward my face. "Good luck," I said, "finding another talented Eskimo with good teeth." And I gave Benno my smile that destroys marriages.

Benno, he tries to talk me out of myself, but this wind remembers who I am.

And now someone is rushing toward me, his head bent to his feet. It's him. The man in the taupe suit. He keeps his eyes on his toes as if he might lose them between the terminal and the plane. This Anchorage wind is not the thin-blade wind of home, but it's a snapping wolf after the wet-dog air of Seattle. And these white men, they have a terrible fear of losing their fingers and their toes when they come this far north.

It happens. Myself, I am descended from a man who lost all twenty. A man from France who woke from freezing to death to find himself pressed naked between the bellies of strangers. People who, when he begged them to put him outside to finish freezing, they just smiled and stuffed his mouth with caribou dipped in seal oil. The women, they laughed and reminded my ancestor that he still had one finger left, the one between his legs. And they made him gloves from seal flippers, so he could paddle his own *umiaq*.

My people.

This wind, it blows me back into myself. And now it has made me invisible. The man in the taupe suit, he does not see me. I am fully exposed in these ugly lights, but he sees only his fear of the wind, his straight line into the plane. I step to the side and he passes me, close enough to touch, but this is not the time for touching. I put my hands in the loose Carhartts' pockets. I keep my thoughts. My thoughts see me under the stars with my people, my hands in fur-lined mittens, my feet in mukluks. My thoughts see me warm in my caribou parka.

I look out from my thoughts and the man in the taupe suit has disappeared into the small plane. And I am the only passenger still out in the wind. Someone puffed out in fluorescent orange is waving me over to climb the steps. His arm is as impatient as the color of his snowsuit. My boot is barely off the metal grill of the top step before he rolls the stairs out from under the plane.

***

The man in the taupe suit, he had his eyes shut and didn't see me come in and take the seat next to him. Never even bothered to look at who he was next to. And now he's asleep. I know he's asleep from the open sprawl of his legs, his bent neck, the sound of his breathing.

We could be in bed together, that's how close his breath is to my ear.

I can smell his itchy scalp problem, the extra-strength dandruff shampoo that smells like road construction. I look down at his package, I've seen better. I look up at his head. His hair is gray as a wolf's, it makes him look older than his face. Myself, I can pass for a minor if that's what a man wants. But my thoughts say that's not what this man wants, this man follows a straight line. And now I must stop looking. My eyes can be as loud as drums in the night, and I don't want him to wake up. Not yet.

This man, I know who he is. I know what he's doing here.

The man in the taupe suit sleeps through take-off. He sleeps through the plane climbing. He does not see the green dancer outside the plane window, what they call Northern Lights. I look around the plane. The plane is almost dark inside, everyone asleep or trying to get there. Myself, I want to meet the man in his dream, I want to meet him in the dark, thousands of feet up in the air.

But not yet. I cover my lap with a blanket and close my eyes. The sound of the engine pulls me under and holds me where I am just enough asleep to let certain things happen, but not so far gone as to be lost.

I know where I am, and I know what I'm doing.

I know I am on a twin-engine plane somewhere above what they call the Arctic Circle, and I know that the air outside this plane is too thin for a man to breathe. I know that the rivers and lakes below us are safely frozen, and I know that if I were down there, I would pull my animal skins around me and long for the feel of a man.

I let my head fall to his shoulder. He stops breathing, and every bone in his body is set to listen. My face is on his expensive wool. I make a small sound, warm as a sleeping puppy, then roll my cheek over the round bone of his shoulder, until I feel his bones go tender enough to feed a baby.

"It's you," he says in a voice just right for the intimacy of a night flight.

The up and down, the in and out of his breathing. The medicated road construction smell of his scalp problem. The heated smell trapped inside his expensive wool. This man, I know what he needs. I know what it takes to wake him all the way up.

And I know why he's here.

Still, I will let him touch me. It's why I spread the blanket across my lap. So his hand can visit in secret.

Wedding ring or no wedding ring, his hand wants to visit in secret.

And it does. His hand enters through the side of my easy-access overalls. His hand enters under my red silk shirt. How he shows his class is he doesn't grab for a nipple. How he shows his class is he doesn't dig down to my crotch. He touches his fingers to the flesh of my belly, and this is the moment. This is the moment all other moments lead up to. The moment when yearning becomes touch. His hand soft on my belly. But then his hand is gone from my belly, his hand is outside pushing my shoulder.

He's pushing me away.

But only to lift the armrest that separates us. Now the hand is back in through the side, under my shirt. I soften the muscles of my belly. And again I fall limp to his shoulder, still pretending I am not fully awake.

My thoughts are fully awake. The man is a stranger, but I know who he is. He is a front line player, one of the nameless suits who fly to my home because of the oil. As for myself, tomorrow I will stand with my people and say no to his plans. In the thin light of day the oil will rise between us—he may or may not recognize me in my caribou parka—but for tonight the oil will stay buried where it has been forever.

Soon enough he will know all my secrets, but first he will love me.

The blanket slides across my leg, he is covering himself with my blanket. The sound I make is for his ears only, low so as not to wake the other passengers. I twist my face on his shoulder, my mouth open to the taste of expensive wool.

The plane flies us among drifting dancers, deep into darkness.

And now I am eyes-open awake, done with pretending to be asleep. I put my hand over his hand, press his wedding ring into the flesh of my belly. My middle finger rubs smooth gold. His hand strains to touch a nipple. I hold tight and whisper *wait*. I breathe the word, moist and warm in his ear. I take his hand away from the elastic of my underpants and out the side of my Carhartts.

Wait.

And now it is my hand that goes to work on his suit. I unzip his pants, undo the button. My hand is calm, my mind steady. He's wearing boxer shorts, I pull out his cock through the slot. His hands grab hold of my hair, he pulls my head to his chest. He pulls, then lets go of my hair. Strokes the length of my hair, all the way down my back.

With my head against his chest, my ear is open to his heart. I hear things he will never say. Not even to himself. I hear that this is all he ever really wanted, this silent straight-forward love, but somehow it all got so complicated.

My hand is not rubbing, my hand is calm. My hand wants only to hold this man where he is most naked.

Wait, I tell him one more time.

I open my mouth and press my full lips around the hollow at the center of his chest. I breathe through his buttoned shirt, blow my hot Eskimo breath into the hollow at the center of his chest. I know what it takes to wake up a man.

Now something is happening. Now something is shaking from the inside out. Now I fill him with the wide-open tundra, waves of caribou into the hollow at the center of his chest. Now I breathe a sky of migrating birds into the hollow at the center of his chest.

I hear him hold back a cry from deep inside himself. I feel him come, hot against the inner skin of my wrist.

Myself, I can't hold him back any longer. His hand wants back inside my pants, it wants between my legs. And I will give this, I will give him what I have between my legs.

But first, I put one finger on the far side of his chin and turn his face to me.

My steady hand, my calm mind.

I need to see his eyes. The airplane lights are dim, but I can still see through his eyes. His eyes are full of pussy, warm and oily. But I don't hate him for this, and I don't want him to hate me. I want our eyes to hold us together in the moment, the moment when everything is out in the open. His see-through eyes, mine dark as night.

His hand bumps my cock. My cock is fully awake, pushing hard against my stretch underwear. His face is not pleased.

This is the moment that all other moments lead up to.

This is wolf in a leghold trap. See-through wolf eyes, the moment before wolf gets what just happened. The man gets what just happened, his eyes are knives in the dark. Before he can do damage, I'm holding on strong to both his wrists.

Thousands of feet up in the air like this, things could go either way.

To This Day

I'm following a matched set of nudes, two silver playgirls in profile, one on each mudflap of the semi up ahead. The road is curvy and splotched with black ice. I don't dare pass. The girls have lost their luster under a film of grime. They're bare-ass and facing each other, heads tossed, big wavy hair, comic book breasts. You just know the hair would be blonde. Naked women in this weather, they make me turn the heater fan a notch higher.

This is Nevada.

A highway sign says how many miles it is to a certain town where Ruby and I stayed the summer I was eighteen. The man who did what he did to me in that town must be dead by now. So many years ago, and he was old when he did it.

All I can get out here is talk radio. The radio man is saying Democrats want to give children access to pornography in public schools.

The man who did what he did to me could have been someone's grandfather. Except for how he smelled. It was odd; why would a man that age wear so much cologne or aftershave? And then I knew. The moment his hand went to his fancy silver belt buckle, I knew it all, even though no one had done such a thing to me before.

The radio man is saying Democrats want pornography in libraries.

I was just a girl, but my sudden understanding was ancient. I knew what that man was about to do to me. There was no thought of escape.

The radio is playing an ad I've already heard a half-dozen times. That innocent looking chip will spread and destroy your entire windshield. But don't despair, you *do* have a choice. If you hurry right in to Hank's Auto Glass you can save yourself the heartache of a costly windshield replacement in the future.

I've got a crack growing in my windshield. Dad pointed it out day before yesterday, just before I left Tucson. I was loading my things, but Dad just had to inspect my car before he'd let me head back to Alaska. Mom was there too, trying to give me more than I had room for—dates, pecans, egg salad sandwiches.

Mom always tries to give me more than I have room for.

Why would anyone want to live in Alaska? Dad said. Look at me and your mom, he said. He put both his arms around Mom. Mom tilted her head so it rested on Dad's shoulder. They posed like that, under the hot Arizona sun, as if I were taking snapshots. Just a couple of old newlyfleds from Wisconsin, Dad said. Wouldn't you rather live where it's warm? Mom said. Why just imagine, patio living year round! Mom's hand swept the prickly pear and gravel yard. Don't tell me you're happy up there, she said. She gave my car a dirty look. I don't care how beautiful the scenery is, you need *family* to be happy. You need people you can laugh and cry with.

I crammed containers of unwanted food into the trunk between my sleeping bag and tent.

You always were a self-contained child, Mom went on, but you had the sweetest laugh. Like snowmelt in spring. Didn't I always say she had the sweetest laugh, Daddy? Didn't I always say she had the laughter of spring?

Mom put her hand in Dad's trouser pocket. She took out his white hanky and pressed it to the wrinkles under her eyes.

The crack on my windshield has definitely grown since Tucson. Maybe if everyone had mudflaps these things wouldn't happen.

The man who did what he did to me didn't bother to wear a rubber. This was before AIDS.

The radio man is saying Democrats have no tolerance for other people's moral values.

I never even cried. When he was done, the man who did what he did to me said, Get out of town and don't come back. I had to lean on his desk to get my panties over my sandals. When my panties were in place, he held the door open. I walked out, right past the Chief of Police, who stood guard outside the door. I kept my eyes on the chief's cowboy boots, each boot tip in a neat line with the crease in his trousers.

Back at the cabin, I washed with Dr. Bronner's soap, straight from the bottle. It stung so bad, it took all my strength to keep silent.

Something smells wrong in my car. I don't think it's me, it's that semi up ahead. His brakes or transmission. I have to gear down to second to keep from tailgating. It sounds like I'm straining my engine. I need to pee anyway, so I stop at a pullout and squat behind a bush. I wipe with a handful of clean snow. I like how the snow bites. When I'm done, the snow in my hand is stained pink. Back at the car I look in my purse, glove box, duffel bag. I can't find a tampon.

The man who did what he did to me was annoyed to find me a virgin. When he was done, he got a white handkerchief out of his pocket and wiped himself. Jesus, he said. He threw his blood-stained handkerchief in the trash.

I can't find a tampon, which means I'll have to stop in that town. I stuff a Kleenex in my underwear. I look at my face in the rearview mirror. Wrinkles on my face, cracks on my windshield.

Fuck it all.

I pull out on the highway.

The kids I got stoned with in that town wouldn't recognize me at this age. I wouldn't know them either, not that I ever did. How it was, a bunch of us would get high, and they'd all clump together like tumbleweeds on a fence. I'd wander off alone into the empty space between things. I'd steep myself in starlight and silence, while their voices rasped in the distance. I could always tell where Ruby was from how she laughed. Ruby's laugh was as big as her belly.

Ruby.

I never told Ruby I went to see the judge. I never told Ruby what that judge did to me. It was bad enough that Ruby went to prison and lost custody of her kids. I didn't want her to blame herself for what happened to me, but that's not why I didn't tell her. I've never told anyone, to this day.

The radio man is taking a call from a woman who listens to his show every chance she gets. I can't thank you enough, the woman says, for having the guts to speak out on behalf of Christian values.

The judge sentenced Ruby to two years. So I called his secretary and made an appointment. Then I had to go to the Salvation Army to find something other than jeans to wear. I bought a yellow sleeveless dress. It hung a couple of inches above my knees. I thought it was the kind of dress you could wear to church, or to an appointment with a judge.

He could have been someone's grandfather. Except for the smell of all that cologne or aftershave.

Is there anything I can do? I said. Anything to help Ruby get out of prison?

He was sitting at his desk, moving books and papers from one end to the other. He stood up and said, All you can do is take this. His hand was on his fancy silver belt buckle. Silver curlicue flowers with gold in the middle, two gold guns with their barrels crossed in a golden X. He undid the buckle. He came to my side of his desk and put his hands on my waist. He turned me like a square dancer, then pushed my butt into the hard edge of his desk. He unzipped his pants. He pulled up my dress and said, Take those off, all the way off. I didn't move. He reached around me and got a long thin letter opener. I can cut them off, if you'd rather, he said. It's your choice, he said. I bent and took off my panties.

He pushed me by the shoulders. He pushed my bare butt into the edge of his desk. He did what he did to me. He said, Get out of town and don't come back.

I took Ruby's van and drove west into a sunset that hurt my eyes. I drove west to California.

California was why Ruby and I had left Madison in the first place, but then her van broke down in Nevada. Ruby's van broke down with nothing in sight for miles around. Nothing but sagebrush and dry distant mountains. It gave

Ruby the creeps, the crusted landscape and dead-looking plants. But I loved the smell of the sage, the dry brilliance of the air after the thick mugginess of Wisconsin. And I liked the way every plant stood alone, with plenty of empty space around it.

The van broke down, and we got out our plastic lawn chairs and sat in its shade. Ruby rolled a joint in a turquoise-colored zigzag. I said, You know, Ruby, how they say that all rivers will eventually flow to the sea? Well, this is the Great Basin. The rivers never get out of here. Ruby said, What rivers?

A local boy drove by in a pickup truck and stopped to help us. Looks to me like you've gone and blown your head gasket, he said. He bent under the van to rope it to his trailer hitch and his pants came down below his butt crack. Ruby winked at me. We had to put our hands over each others' mouths to keep ourselves under control. For the rest of that summer, whenever one of us couldn't stop laughing, the other one would say, Looks to me like you've gone and blown your head gasket.

Ruby always said laughing was the next best thing to sex.

The kid towed the van to the nearest town, into someone's backyard. They said they'd fix it for less than the gas station, but we'd have to wait for parts. Ruby gave them both some mescaline. They invited us to a party. Ruby was generous with her Acapulco Gold that night, especially with this one guy who worked as a firefighter. He took us up into the starlit hills a short distance from town. He showed us a sagging cabin, where he said we could stay as long as we wanted. I liked the idea of a log cabin with no electricity or neighbors. Ruby liked the firefighter. Ruby finally had someone who would sleep with her between her gold satin sheets, since I never would.

The radio man is saying Democrats want to promote homosexuality in the classroom.

From the time I started babysitting her kids back in Madison, Ruby was always inviting me to her gold satin sheets. I'd never heard of bisexuals back then. I thought she was just being overly polite. She'd come home from the motel room where she met her art professor, and I'd be almost asleep, in my flannel pajamas, on her couch. She'd say, Are you sure? Wouldn't you rather be in a queen-size bed with satin sheets? No, I'm fine, thanks. Well, have you ever even *tried* satin sheets? No, I'm comfortable right here. Really. Go to bed. The next morning I'd wake up all cramped on the couch, to the noise of morning cartoons and the smell of crepes frying in butter. Once it was a fondue pot full of burping chocolate, with Ruby at the kitchen table, fat and naked under her silk kimono, plucking leaves off strawberries.

It's starting to snow. This snow will stay trapped here forever. Even after it melts, it won't ever make it to the ocean. The snowflakes swirl into the windshield like I'm at the helm of a spaceship. All alone and drifting. I could use a cup of coffee.

Back then we used Dexedrine to stay awake. Ruby told me how anyone could go to student health and get diet pills, you didn't even have to be fat like her. So I got a prescription. I used the Dex to pull all-nighters. I was always a straight-A student, even before diet pills. Ruby said she could tell I was smart from the first time she laid eyes on me in Geology 101. That's why I was the one she chose from an auditorium full of freshmen. She waited for me near the door of the lecture hall, this big Nordic woman with too much makeup and a brassy Afro that made her look even bigger. I couldn't believe she wanted to talk to *me*.

You look like someone who can help me, Ruby said. I'm one of those prom night statistics, Ruby said. Prom night? I said. Yeah, Ruby said, it was in *Reader's Digest*. Prom night is the most probable night to, one, lose your virginity, two, get pregnant. Then the boy's parents made us get married, and then we had another one, and now I'm divorced and on welfare. Really, this is not an interesting story, Ruby said, but it's why I'm in over my head with this whole university thing. So can you teach me how to study?

I went home with Ruby and she offered me pot. It was my first time. I don't feel anything, I said. Ruby choked on the smoke, as though I'd said something funny. What did you do to your hair? I asked. You look like Brunhilda of the jungle. Ruby cracked up, then brought out her home perm kits and dyes. Ruby wanted to bleach me into a blonde on the spot. But all I wanted to do was eat Ruby's homemade biscuits with cream cheese and apple butter.

Ruby took Dexedrine to try and make up for her binges. She'd pick up a dozen Dunkin Donuts after her art professor had to go home to his wife. He always left Ruby hungry for more. And there I was on her couch when she got home, pretending to be asleep. Since I'd never join her between her satin sheets, she had to eat the donuts in bed all by herself.

A road sign says Great Basin National Park next right, but it's got to wait 'til I get some tampons.

There was no Great Basin National Park the summer Ruby and I lived here. Wanting to see the new park, especially the bristlecone pines, is why I'm driving this way instead of Interstate 5 through California. But it's snowing. You'd think May would be all wildflowers and spring in the

Lower 48. I drive over the last summit, then it's downhill the rest of the way into town.

The judge said, Don't come back. But I need tampons.

He did what he did to me, then he said, Get out of town and don't come back. So I loaded our stuff from the cabin into Ruby's van. I made a small fire of sagebrush wood and tried to burn the yellow dress and my blood-soaked panties. The panties caught fire, but the dress just melted. It put black smoke in the air. The smoke smelled like poison.

I drove all afternoon and into the night, until I crossed the state line into California. It was cold up in the Sierras. I pulled off the road by a river that *would* make it to the sea, and I checked twice to make sure all the doors were locked. I closed the curtains and lit a candle. I put Ruby's gold satin sheets on the foam pad that covered the floor of the van. I put Ruby's red satin comforter over her gold satin sheets. Ruby's gold satin sheets were ice against my skin. But they smelled like coconut and vanilla. They smelled like Ruby. I opened up my sleeping bag and spread it over Ruby's red comforter. Still, I shivered all night.

The radio man is talking about the liberal media. He's getting all wound up. I push the seek button. The radio seeks but it does not find anything but where I started. Now it's weather on the hour. The weather man says to expect more snow. I turn the radio off.

I might as well be in Alaska.

But why must you live in Alaska? Mom couldn't leave it alone. So cold up there, she said. Worse than Wisconsin. And how will you ever meet anyone living in a place with more bears than men? Well Mom, maybe I like bears better than men. Nonsense, she said. Look at me and Daddy. You just haven't found the right man. You never give yourself a chance. You should try smiling more. You have such a pretty smile. I wouldn't say this if I didn't love you, but you should look in a mirror. Practice smiling. No man will want a woman who doesn't know how to laugh or smile. And don't tell me you're too old for a man, you've still got half your life ahead of you. Why I'd even be relieved if you told me you preferred women! You're not one, are you? One what, Mom? No, Mom, I'm not a lesbian. I'm not anything, Mom. Well, I don't care if you are, I just want you to be happy. Don't you want to be happy, sweetie? I don't know, Mom. I guess I never thought about it. I like Alaska. All that empty space.

Well, you always were a self-contained child.

I never told anyone. They say you're supposed to talk about these things. But I always *was* a self-contained child. And then I was a woman. Just like that, the moment the judge's hand went to unbuckle his belt.

Ruby had just been sentenced. She'd been busted in a sting operation. They called her Judith in court. Judith Irene Nelson. A narc testified against her. This guy, who we believed was our friend. This guy who we all believed was a rock hunter from up in the Snake Mountains. He stood up in court and swore to tell the truth and nothing but the truth. Yes, the defendant Judith Irene Nelson sold him an ounce of marijuana. The bottom half of his face was white where he'd shaved off his beard. He'd cut off his long hair too. He wore a suit. I'd never seen him in anything but jeans and buckskin.

This was a guy who, one night when everyone was partying, watched me walk away into the empty space between things. He followed me out there. We sat on the ground and smoked hash from a soapstone pipe. He said he'd carved the pipe himself. He gave me a crystal. It's from a cave, he said, up by the bristlecones. The crystal was moonglow in the palm of my hand. Bristlecone pines are the oldest trees on the planet, he said. He put his arms around me, and I let him. I liked the wild smoky smell of his buckskin. Maybe some day I'll take you up there to see them, he said. How old? I asked. Thirty this year, he said. No, not you, the trees. Well, he said, the Forest Service cut one down so they could count the rings. Four-thousand and nine-hundred of them. That one turned out to be the oldest living tree on earth, he said.

I tried to see his face in the moonlight.

But it's dead, I said.

I let him kiss me. His mustache poked inside my nose.

What this narc did later that summer, is he got Ruby to sell him a lid of Acapulco Gold. Ruby wasn't the only one selling stuff. Local kids were pushing cocaine, acid, meth. You name it. They all got busted, but Ruby was the only one sentenced to serve time.

So I went to see the judge.

He knew I was coming. I was punctual. The police chief was in there, in the judge's chambers. I recognized the police chief from court. He was another one who tried to make it look like Ruby had something to do with all the drugs in town. He and the judge were laughing about something when I showed up for my appointment. I stood outside the open door. The judge stopped laughing as soon as he saw me standing there. The chief turned and looked at my yellow dress. The dress was above my knees, but not *that* short. Someone was wearing too much cologne or after-shave. The judge told the chief to wait outside the door. This won't take but a minute or two, he said. He moved the books and papers from one end of his desk to the other. The chief closed the door behind him. Is there anything I can do? I said. Anything to help Ruby get out of prison? All you can do is take this, he said. And he stood up and put his hand on his fancy belt buckle.

The police chief waited outside the door. He waited for the judge to finish.

Get out of town and don't come back, the judge said. And then, while I was trying to get my sandals back through the legs of my panties without tipping over, he said something else. He said, Things could go real bad for your girlfriend in prison. I finally got both feet through. I tried to wipe the blood up my legs as I pulled on my white cotton panties.

Or maybe not so bad, the judge said to my back. I walked out. I walked past the police chief.

Your choice, the judge said behind me. He said it lightly, the way you'd say, Take care.

I'm almost to the edge of town now. Nothing's changed. Except for a Texaco Truck Plaza that wasn't here twenty-seven years ago. A sign says Free Coffee. I park and step out of my car into the cold wet wind, then go inside and buy tampons. I don't look at the guy who takes my money. I go to the bathroom. I don't look at my face in the mirror.

All they have with the free coffee is powdered non-dairy creamer. I take my free coffee black and leave town. Once out, I turn up the radio. The radio is saying if I don't deal with that chip in my windshield *now*, it will spread and destroy—I smack the knob with the end of my fist. Silence. I drive all the way back to the junction for Great Basin National Park. I pull off the road and find the magazine article I've carried all this way. The article says the oldest bristlecone pine trees are found where climatic and geologic conditions are harshest. The article says they've had all but a few inches of living bark blasted away by wind and ice, but that this thin strip sustains life. The article calls them ancient fighters, survivors in epic struggles that toughen them for longevity.

The judge has got to be dead. He was old enough to be somebody's grandfather. His cologne or aftershave smelled worse than what you use to clean a toilet. I tried to hold my breath while he did what he did to me.

The narc was supposed to be the first one.

He was supposed to be a mountain man who hunted rocks for a living. He said that when he killed a deer he used every part of it. He said his shirt was so soft because he'd tanned the hide with the deer's own brain. He said he used sagebrush to smoke the hide. I loved to breathe in the smell, deep and slow, when he held me close. He took me to some hot springs and we kissed naked in the hot slippery water. His lips and tongue were warm. His mouth was so wet and soft, it made me want to touch him in places I'd never touched anyone. And I wanted him to touch me. He said my breasts were exquisite. Not too small? I said. No, perfect, he said. Of course, I've never met a breast I didn't like, he said.

He made me laugh. I didn't mind that he'd had other girlfriends before. It made me feel special, that I was the one he was with now.

Your laugh, he said, it's like water in the desert.

I thought he was a mountain man. His long hair, his beard, his buckskin.

I'd love to be the first to have you, he said, but only if you're sure. Are you sure? he said. I'm sure, I said. I was afraid to look at it, but I touched what he was promising me. I touched it in the hot slippery water. Will it hurt? I said. And he said, A juicy thing like you? If it hurts you at all, he said, I guarantee it will only be for a moment.

I went to the clinic. I sat in the waiting room with the Indian women and their pregnant daughters. I got a prescription and started taking birth control pills.

He promised to bring me up here and show me the bristlecone pine trees. My first time was supposed to be with a mountain man. Outside, under the moon and the stars, on a blanket of buckskin. That smell I could never get enough of.

It was only supposed to hurt for a moment.

My mouth falls open. I spill free coffee on the caption, *Tortured and Twisted Shapes*. The free coffee is bitter and cold. I roll down the window and dump what's left. Now the snow is falling in heavy wet clumps. I promised myself bristlecones, but the road won't be open up there, not with all this snow.

We were planning a camping trip. He said he came from the mountains. And me, I've always been partial to mountains.

It's how I ended up in Alaska.

Mountains aren't enough, Mom said. You show me the mountain that can love you back. Where did you lose your laugh? You seem so distant. Please, I'm your mother.

That judge was old enough to be someone's grandfather. He put his hand on his fancy silver and gold belt buckle. Such an odd place for a judge's hand to go when you've come to ask for help. When I went into his chambers, I was afraid he'd point his finger at me and give me a lecture about drugs. I was ready to say yes sir, no sir in all the right places. Or maybe he'd throw his hands in the air and say, Your friend can't be helped. See what happens when you break the law?

But his hand went to his belt. A girl cannot know the

things I knew from watching his hand. That girl stopped breathing, and who breathed through her body instead was someone else. Someone ancient and weary.

I stared at the mountains outside the window until he was done. I was already gone. Safe and alone in the dry distant mountains.

TAYLOR HAWKE

Sitting here on the edge of an exam table, loud paper under my bare butt, wearing nothing but the moccasins on my feet. I sit naked and I wait. Until I have to close my eyes against the fluorescent lights of this windowless room. Against the poster before me on the wall, against its bug's eye view of epidermal carcinomas. I wait and I try to pretend the patience I have when I'm waiting for a deer or a fish. Try to pretend the chill on my skin is real air and not the stale draft from an air conditioner. And just when I'm ready to hop down, to put on my skins and free myself from all this, here is a woman. She immediately draws back as if she's opened the door on the wrong room.

"Didn't the nurse give you a gown?" she says.

I point my thumb over my shoulder at the unopened throwaway on the exam table. It hadn't occurred to me that the doctor would be female, much less good-looking, but I know enough to keep my mouth shut on both counts.

She stands in the doorway a moment longer, sniffs the air, then her eyes land on the chair where I've left my smoked buckskins. She steps in and closes the door behind her. As much as I can see, she's got a nice slender body. When did they start making doctors so young? She lifts the beard that covers half my chest. Her eyes dismiss various moles and spots on my skin, then notice the gouge to the side of my belly. She drops the beard and touches a fingertip to the white scar tissue. "What's this?" she says.

"Bullet," I say. I reach over my shoulder and tap the flat leech-like thing on my back. "I'm here about this," I say.

She steps to my side and looks, then has me stand and turn around. I feel her eyes on my butt, the backs of my legs. "Okay," she says, and I return to the edge of the table.

"We won't really know anything until we get the biopsy results," she says, her eyes aimed at a corner of the room where I'm not. I don't know who this woman is, some dermatologist I found in the yellow pages. Her own skin as pale and indifferent to seasons as the air in this room. She obviously lives by the teachings in her lobby. Pamphlets with titles like "Our Sun: The Star that Burns."

"Please," I say.

She swabs something icy over the spot on my back.

"You can be up front with me." I attempt a laugh, it comes out a grunt. "I sense that you're holding back."

She moves one of my braids and injects a needle behind my shoulder. I keep my breath casual, as if I don't feel the pierce or the fluid she's plunging into me. Then she steps away and pushes the empty hypo through a trash slot under the counter. What a waste, all this waste generated by my coming to this place, from the bleached paper I'm sitting on to her disposable gloves. I should never have come.

"Us blue-eyed Caucasians need to cover up when we're in places like Nevada," she says, still facing the sink. "Tanned skin is damaged skin," she goes on. "And the way that thing looks—the color, the ragged edges…" She turns and moves to my side, she touches my back, and although that area is numb, I imagine her pale fingertips tracing around the black stain she's about to slice off.

"I wish you hadn't waited so long to have this checked." She steps back in front of me, finally aims her blue eyes at mine. "It looks like malignant melanoma," she says. "It's quite possible it already metastasized."

I lower my eyes to the steel edge of the blade she's holding. "If it weren't so awkward to reach," I say, "I would've cut that thing out myself." The area is numb by now, yet I sense the weight of her hand on my shoulder, the pressure of her cutting.

"With a fresh flake of obsidian," I go on. "A good quality obsidian blade will slide right between the cells. A steel blade rips its way through."

"Sorry," she says, "All I've got is stainless steel."

She finishes and presses a Band-aid to my back, then goes back to the counter. I get off the table and step into my buckskin pants. I don't want to see the thing she cut from my flesh.

"Melanoma," I say. "It sounds like a name for a beautiful woman."

The doctor takes off her gloves and pushes them through the trash slot. "You're that guy I read about in the paper." She turns and faces me. "Ex-cop turned wilderness guru?"

I pull my buckskin shirt over my head, bury my face in the wild smoky smell, then push my head through, back to the foreign light of the room.

"Did they run that article again?" I say. "Every year or so this town runs out of news and someone at the paper recycles the old Taylor Hawke story." I pull my braids out over my shirt. We stand and look at each other under the cruel light.

"This is going to kill me, right?" I say.

She hands me a glossy brochure from the pile on her counter. "I'm sorry, Mr. Hawke," she says, turning to leave, "I'm not an oncologist."

Outside the refrigerated clinic, the sudden blast of heat from the pavement makes me feel drunk, tempts me to curl up on the hot sidewalk for a nap. Instead I climb into my open-air jeep and leave town. I race toward the watery mirage where the road meets the hot summer sky, that just-out-of-reach shimmering lake. Then I leave the highway with its stink of tar and diesel and turn onto a gravel road that winds up and up and up into the mountains. Eventually I'm following no more than a pair of tire tracks through the sage. As I gain elevation the air grows clean and cool, until after a couple of hours, I'm on the washed-out canyon trail that leads home to Cottonwood Creek. And at the campfire that evening I do not speak of what happened in town. I look into the fire-lit faces of the seekers who have come here to learn aboriginal life skills, and I give them the stories they want. As if it were possible to go back.

A soapstone pipe is making the rounds, and when it comes into my hands I touch the heated bowl, carved into some kind of primitive face, filled with smoldering bud. I make a show of admiring the craftsmanship of the kid who carved it, then pass it on without toking. I stand and reach into the pocket of my buckskin pants to pull out the stiff paper that's poking me there. The green-haired girl who calls herself Juniper is watching my every move with her doe eyes. There's a Juniper in every group, some girl who will want to stay on after the others return to their cities or migrate south for the winter. Some girl who thinks I'm her fantasy, whose idea of romance is winter in a tipi. This one is trying to see what's on the glossy brochure in my hand. I quickly toss it into the fire, let the flames eat those vulgar close-ups. The paper flames up green and blue and violet, colors that could be seen as lovely if you were high on pot or if you didn't suspect they were caused by something toxic in the ink.

***

Cottonwood Creek is wild with spring. Winter snow is melting off the mountaintops, but at this elevation the snow has been replaced by drifts of white fluff from the cottonwoods. I'm on the sitting stone outside the door of my tipi while Juniper stands behind me and braids my hair, something she started doing for me at the end of winter when I lost control of my right arm. Her hands are angry this morning.

"Juniper," I say, "what are you so pissy about?"

"Why should I tell you anything about me if you won't tell me anything about you." She yanks my braids as firmly as if weaving a watertight basket.

I open my eyes to the brilliance of the morning sun, bathe my face in its fire. "There are two kinds of brain cancer," I say, "meatballs and sauce. Meatballs are operable, I've got sauce."

Juniper's hands stop moving in my hair. "Taylor," she says, "what are you saying?"

"I'm telling you what the oncologist told me."

Juniper leans into me, the back of my head between her naked breasts, the rise and fall of her breath. "What about chemo?" she says.

I close my eyes, try to hear the music of Cottonwood Creek.

Juniper crosses her arms over my chest, rests her cheek on my head. "Taylor, Taylor, Taylor," she says, her voice soft. As if she could shush away the nightmare. Then she straightens up and gently ties off the end of the last braid.

I reach down and take her wrist with my one good hand, pull her around to stand in front of me where I can nuzzle her breasts with my tongue and my nose and my lips. I press my ear to her ribs and feel the beating of her heart. Juniper's body is as fresh and warm as the sun on my face.

She holds my head in her hands for a moment, then wraps her fingers around the tops of my braids and pulls my face back. "I think you'd look better bald," she says, her sad brown eyes.

"Okay, then," I say, "I'll shave my head for you. You want me to lose the beard too?"

She tightens her grip as if my braids are ropes she wants to climb. "You don't even know for sure it would fall out," she says. "Not everyone loses their hair, and if you do, I'll shave my head too." Juniper's short messy hair with its dead green tips and a winter's growth of lush dark roots.

"Juniper," I say.

She lets go of my braids, then shakes her head sadly and walks off. Her flawless back, the rise and fall of her hips under a pair of low-slung jeans. I breathe it all in and out, then offer my face again to the rising sun.

No, this is where the music stops. These mountains, this creek, this girl.

But not just yet. The day is filled with the movement of spring. So many sounds to Cottonwood Creek at this time of year. I can sort them out, match each sound to what the water's doing to make it—a spout dropping off the edge of a stone, the slow gurgle of an eddy, a quick riffling over rocks like the sound of a girl's laughter.

A certain girl's laughter. Who was that girl? We were bathing together at the hot springs. A certain overly serious girl, I wanted to make her laugh for the pure pleasure it gave my ears. And now I seem to remember her breasts, smaller than Juniper's. She was so bashful to have me see, much less touch them. She was worried they weren't the right size, but I told her I'd never met a breast I didn't like, and yes, that was what set off her laughter. A laugh so clear it made my line seem fresh and original. How is it I can remember a laugh, but not a face or a name?

But I do not want this other girl with me now, not when I have so little time left. I open my eyes to the luminous morning. I will go to the creek and splash its icy water on my face. I stand and here is a tingle in my leg, reminiscent of the tingle that was in my arm before it became a dead limb. And now my terror is a crow unfolding its black wings inside my chest.

***

Streamers of tiny air bubbles snake up from the hot mud, up the inside of my one leg that still works. They tickle a trail up my balls like a shy girl's fingertips. I arch my back, my feet release from the mud, and now I'm floating in the hot sulfurous water. I stretch myself out and float with my ears submerged, utterly alone in my failed body. I close my eyes and drift backwards in time, back to when it was good, back to a girl who wrapped her smooth young legs around me, who softened herself to my embrace, then drifted on. A drifting girl, and this was a good thing, this giving and taking of pleasure, the sound of a girl's laughter.

I break free of the thick suffocating water, suddenly too hot to bear, emerge to the gurgle and trill of a thousand redwing blackbirds. Juniper jerks her head up from whatever dream she's been dreaming at the far edge of this hole. "Do you want to get out?" she says. She swim-walks toward me, her arms trying to push the obstructing water aside.

Yes, I want out! Out of this stinking mudhole, out of this misfiring brain, out of this miserable ending. My mind is screaming all this, but all that come out is a weak yes.

Juniper crawls onto the bank and kneels above me. Mud streams from her patch, down the smooth skin between her thighs. She bends and reaches down under the water and hooks her hand into the belt around my waist, and with the help of my one arm and my one leg that still works, she hoists me onto the muddy bank. I sit on the edge, naked but for the harness belt, my feet in the water, and I wait. The nearby marshes are swollen with blackbirds, their dark silhouettes swaying the tips of the reeds as they land, then take off again, free to fly where they want.

Juniper goes into the shallow side of the pool and washes the mud from between her legs. Her body is burnished by sunset light. What good am I to her? She leaves the water and brings over the wheelchair, sets the brake.

"Do you feel trapped?" I say.

"Not really," she says. "At least I can quit worrying about you running off with another woman." She goes down on one knee and dips her shoulder under my armpit. She's getting stronger by the day, while my muscles turn soft and decompose. She takes me by the belt and helps me stand, nudges her foot under my useless one, and then, with our two legs as one, she walks me the few steps to the wheelchair and lowers me into it. Her breasts are close enough I could touch them with my tongue, but I don't have the appetite for it any more, and what is a man without his appetite?

"So you've got me where you want me," I say. I laugh like a person who's dying.

Juniper pulls loose the sarong that's draped over the back of the wheelchair and flaps it open in the breeze, the color of apricots and tangerines, so many things never to taste again. She wraps the sarong around her waist, then pushes me back along the track I've made across the landscape, where the tire treads of my wheelchair have cracked through the baked crust. My track follows the higher ground at the edge of the marsh, then snakes through the greasewood and sage. It ends at the veranda of a bunkhouse that's held together by cobwebs, all that's left of the Devil's Teapot Ranch.

Juniper turns the wheelchair around and muscles it backwards up the step, then angles the chair, facing me into the flames of sunset.

The screen door squeaks shut, the mountains are dark in the distance. Birds dip into the dying colors of the sky, they come and go over the marsh, they chortle and fuss, all stirred up at the thought of night. Juniper comes back out wearing a sweatshirt over her sarong. She helps me into a pair of loose tie-dyed pants she found at the Salvation Army.

"I wouldn't want to be caught dead in these," I say.

"The only other choice was hospital pants," she says. "That hospital green that orderlies wear? They had plenty of those." She puts a flannel shirt around my back. I get my left arm into one sleeve, while she works my right through the other. I reach up my left hand and grab her sweatshirt by its sleeve.

"Promise me," I say. "Promise me, no hospital."

***

High noon of a hot breathless day and Juniper has left me

wheelchaired out here on the veranda. She fled to town for painkillers. I sent her off in my jeep, told her I could manage for a couple of hours with a jug of water and a pee bucket, out here in the shade.

I sit here fingering the puckered scar near my belly. It occurs to me that this bullet will be all that remains of me centuries after my bones have whitened the dust. One lone bullet. It's been over half a lifetime since this unclaimed bullet came to rest so close to my spine that they said taking it out would risk putting me in a wheelchair. One mystery bullet, shocking in its brilliancy of light against the pale tracery of my ribs, the muted grays of the x-ray, but I walked out of that hospital and there were the holy mountains, solid and real above the stench and traffic of that other world. I walked free into the rest of my life. And then I took to walking barefoot and in winter I wore moccasins and every step was a living event to feel with all my born-again senses.

And now I'm digging my one good hand into the deep pocket of these tie-dyed pants. I find the packet of soft doeskin and unwrap a thumb-size shard of obsidian that I salvaged from my flint knapping pit. A perfect flake. I turn over my limp right arm and stare at the veins I will open. I'm feeling bad about the mess this will make and the mess I made this morning when I woke up with my head in a helmet of pain, and what that pain dredged out of me, the curses and vomit. And Juniper freaking out, forgetting everything she promised and trying to drag me off to town. Me holding on to the bunk's bedpost with my one good arm, shouting, "NO! No hospital! No doctor!" Juniper running out, the sound of her stomping around and crying on the porch, the whooshing sound inside my skull, the feel of my brain choking on itself.

I'm better now. And although I can feel this thing happening inside my head, a certain pressure against my skull, in this moment the pain is tolerable. In this moment I can watch a marsh hawk spread its wings and take off from a fence post to glide low over the reeds. In this moment I can feel the glowing heat of this day, I can yearn toward the slightest breeze, feel its touch on my damp skin.

I hold my perfect obsidian flake to the sky, one edge is almost see-through. I don't want to break or dull the thin blade, so I use the thicker black edge to cut through the drawstring waistband of my pants. This is not an easy thing to do with one hand. I manage to rip and cut and wiggle my way free of the pants. Now there is blood, blood from my hand and from a nick in my belly. Small clean cuts. I hold the blade between my lips, blot the cuts with the tie-dye cloth from the pants, drop the pants to the floor, take the blade from my mouth.

Now I am only waiting for the right moment to finish the job.

One last look out into the throbbing light of day. The marsh hawk's post is still empty. A final look at the mountains, those mountains that have known me better than any woman. In front of the mountains, a slow cloud of white dust moves across the sagebrush. It's too soon for Juniper to be coming back. Whoever it is, they're driving like a tourist. Anyone familiar would be trying to outrace the dust, trailing a rooster-tail plume. I glance at the blade in my fingers and slip it under my thigh.

A white car stops between the two rotting timbers that once held the ranch gate, then creeps up the rutted driveway along the half-dead row of poplars, stops before the ruins of the main house. Sunlight glares off a cracked windshield.

The car door squeaks open and a woman gets out. Short dykey gray hair. She stands, half-hidden by the door of her car, and stares for a few long moments at the remains of the Devil's Teapot Ranch. She comes out a few paces, but it's hard to tell much about her shape with those saggy trousers and that loose work shirt she's wearing. As if it mattered at this point. I'm holding my breath to choke down something that wants to erupt from my mouth. Is it a giggle or a sob that I'm not bleeding to death at this moment, that I can still wonder about the shape of some stranger's body?

She looks around at the collapsed house and outbuildings, the big water tank on the side of the hill out back, shot full of bullet holes. Her eyes follow a trickle of green that starts at the open end of a pipe and trails down to the marsh. She seems to be deliberately not looking at the bunkhouse. That's fine with me, hopefully I'm enough in the shadows she won't spot me. She lifts her hand to shield her eyes, then steps back like she's about to leave. Yes, she should leave and let me finish my work. I twitch my thigh, feel the sharp stone underneath. She seems for a moment to support herself on the open door of the car, then she slowly straightens up, slams it shut, and walks toward me. And even though she's small, her way of walking adds weight to the earth's gravity.

She stops at the step. This close, she's old. She stands there and looks at me like I sold her a lame horse.

"Not many women would walk up to a naked stranger in a wheelchair," I say, just to break the silence.

She eyeballs my dick like it's a pile of rat droppings. Then turns and points west. "You brought me to this place once," she says. "There's some hot springs over there, somewhere on the edge of that marsh." Her hand falls to her side, as dead as mine. She stares off at the distant mountains.

So this is what happened to that girl, she turned into this. What was her name?

"Is it Nora?" I say.

"No," she says.

A lizard skitters onto a large rock. She moves her head to watch it.

"Well," I say. "You gonna tell me?"

"Mona," she says, still watching the lizard.

"Yeah, that's right," I say. "Mona. What's it been, twenty-five, thirty years?"

"I ran into your girlfriend on the road," Mona says. "She flagged me down, asked if I was coming to the hot springs, asked me to keep an eye on you till she got back." Mona comes a step closer, but not onto the porch. She sees the bloody pants on the floor. "You're bleeding," she says.

"It's nothing," I say. "You can go have your soak, if that's what you came for."

She makes no move to leave, just stands defeated under the sun and stares at my pants. "You promised you'd take me to see the bristlecones," she finally says, barely audible, her eyes still on the pants.

"Why did you come here?" I say.

"To see the bristlecones," she says, her voice louder now, but still dull with the effort of speaking.

"You're at the wrong elevation for that," I say.

And now she looks at me, and I get the same feeling as when I come across an abandoned open pit copper mine, all that desolation.

"I already saw them," she says. "You were right about those trees, that's the one thing you didn't lie about."

The lizard is doing pushups on the rock.

"You were supposed to be a mountain man," she says.

"You're right, I was."

There's still a suggestion of what I remember in her face, if I can get past how she is now. She can't be as old as she looks, she's plenty younger than me, and it took dying to make me feel old.

"I'm sorry," I say. "I really did like you, I wanted to be your lover, that part was true. And the rest, what happened to your friend, it wasn't supposed to go that way. It was a local meth dealer I was after. Your friend just got caught up in the bust."

"Ruby never sold anything but pot," Mona says. "You shaved off your beard. You cut your hair. You put on a suit and you testified against her in court." Mona's eyes are low and off to the side, she's watching the lizard. "Ruby lost her kids." Mona's voice is weary beyond blame.

"I quit that job," I say.

"Guess you had to," Mona says to the lizard, "being in a wheelchair."

"This?" My one good fist taps the armrest. "No, this is all new, this is just now happening."

Mona gives me a sudden look. I know I should ask her onto the porch, she's standing there in the hot sun, but I don't have time for this. If I delay much more, I'll have to slice my jugular instead of my veins, and I'd prefer a slow fade. I could shout at her to go, scare her away, but I haven't the heart for it.

"I'd invite you to step up and get out of the sun," I say. "Except that you've come at a really bad time. I was about to cut through some veins here and end my life."

Mona stands there watching the lizard doing pushups. Then she looks at me and I know this face, I know the girl, remember this about her: under the moon, in the sagebrush, sitting on the ground, both of us stoned on hash, and that's when I told her about the bristlecones and how they cut the biggest one down to count the rings, only to find it was the oldest living thing on earth. But the girl didn't laugh like I'd expected, she looked at me in a way that cut straight through the irony of my story, exposing me to a depth of loss I didn't want to feel. It's why I had to kiss her then, just to close her eyes.

And now Mona is starting to waver and break apart in the light, as if she's standing in the watery mirage at the end of the road and something is blowing up inside my head and the lizard is pumping up and down like he's fucking the rock and I want to say something, but I can't, I clutch at my head with my one good hand and the sounds that I hear could only be coming from me.

***

"Taylor Hawke, you are one crazy *taibo*, trying to do brain cancer without drugs."

The stale smell of cigarette smoke. My eyes open and it's Alice John, grinning at me with her stained crooked teeth and pulling a needle out of my arm. Juniper is standing near the edge of the porch. I see someone's covered my cock with the bloody remains of my pants and that my thigh is wrapped with a tie-dyed strip. I reach under and my blade is gone. My hand comes up covered in blood. I must have ground my leg into the blade. But where is it now?

"Where's Mona?" I say.

"She went to the pipe for water," Juniper says. "Who is that woman, Taylor? Did she cut you?"

Alice John pulls the porch's one ratty lawn chair up beside me and sits in it. Half the chair's strapping is busted and trailing to the floor and her butt threatens to break through. She wraps a blood pressure cuff around my good arm, pumps it up.

"Alice," I say. "Find me a lethal dose of something."

Alice concentrates on what she's doing, then pulls loose the cuff. "Can't do that, Hawke," she says. "Sorry."

"I'll get on my knees for you, Alice, if I can."

Alice leans back in the chair, lets out a smoke-scarred laugh. "I better go find me a camera," she says. "Taylor Hawke on his knees before Alice John. The man who trades in his women the way most *taibos* do cars."

Juniper turns away.

"I'm serious, Alice," I say.

"Maybe you could go to Oregon," she says. "They got that Death with Dignity deal." Then she shakes her head and says, "No, that won't work, you gotta be a legal resident."

"Something, Alice, anything. Ask around on the rez, I'll make a trade. I've got some primo brain-tanned hides worth seven or eight hundred dollars, my tipi up on Cottonwood Creek, a couple of bows."

"Still out-Indianing the Indians," Alice says.

"My jeep," I say.

"That jeep is older than your girlfriend," Alice says. She nods toward Juniper.

I sag back into the wheelchair, close my eyes. And now I'm so sleepy, fading into a dream. A young Alice, lean and feisty, home for the summer from nursing school. Those unruly teeth.

"Alice," I say. "Did we ever get around to fucking?" Footsteps on the porch, the sound of water, sloshing, dripping, a wet cloth on my forehead, my belly, the distant sound of a girl crying, Juniper, off at the far end of the porch.

"Get me out of here, Alice," I whisper.

***

The smell of beans and onions and wood smoke. I wake up on the lower bunk, sweating under the flannel lining of an old sleeping bag. A candle burns in a tuna can on an upturned wooden crate. From the other room comes the sound of a lid rattling over a boiling pot on the woodstove. The floor creaks and here is Juniper, pushing through the flimsy gauze she hung in the doorway. She's wearing the doeskin dress I made for her. I kick free with my one good leg, kick the sleeping bag to the floor.

"Alice says you need a hospital bed," Juniper says. "She thinks she can get it through hospice."

I shake my head no.

"You're in denial," Juniper says. She gets the sleeping bag off the floor and puts it on the top bunk, then sits in the wheelchair next to the bed.

"No," I say. "You're the one in denial."

"I don't want us to fight," Juniper says. "Let's get you dressed."

"No," I say. "Just take me out."

Juniper puts the harness belt around my waist, gets me into the chair, and wheels me out naked. She leaves me alone long enough to remember how cold this desert can get after sundown, then comes back outside with a lit kerosene lantern and a large shopping bag. She sets the lantern on the rail and from the bag she pulls out a corduroy shirt and something else.

"Look what else I found for you while I was waiting for Alice," she says. She unfolds some kind of loosely knit blanket.

"What's that?" I say.

"It's a coverlet," she says. "Totally crocheted by hand, I thought you'd appreciate that." She helps me into the corduroy shirt, then tucks the coverlet under my armpits, around my thighs. This thing that looks like it was made by someone in a nursing home.

A coverlet! I should never have let Juniper bring me down from the mountains, down to the cow-blasted ruins of this ranch, this place at the end of a road where anyone can drive up on a whim.

"What's she still doing here?" I say, nodding my head at the ghost of Mona's white car, still parked where she left it, moonlight caught in the cracks of her windshield.

"She went for a soak with Alice," Juniper says. "I invited them to stay for supper. She'll be driving Alice back to town after we eat." Juniper lowers herself into the torn lawn chair. Her fingers start braiding the long fringe on the yoke of her dress.

"I never knew you and Alice were lovers." She pulls apart the braided fringe. "Did you fuck Mona too? Do you fuck every woman you ever meet?"

"Not any more," I say.

Juniper gives me a look. She takes the lantern and goes inside. I sit in the dark and think about my perfect flake of obsidian and how I can get it back.

***

They're all looking at me from down the long plank table, their kerosene-lit eyes, Alice and Juniper on one side, Mona alone on the opposite bench. They've all three stopped eating and are now watching me lose it in my wheelchair at the head of the table. I'm lifting chili by the spoonful and dumping it into my beard. And this is something new, this is not my hand failing, this is my brain. I see this, see that my brain is giving faulty instructions to my one good hand. I sit here with my spoon suspended, and I stare at the grease stained wood. Then try to laugh, as if this were funny.

Juniper goes for the dishrag and dips it into the water bucket. She wrings it out and comes over to clean my beard. Then sits at the end of the bench and takes the spoon from my hand, begins to feed me. Alice gets up and starts opening cabinets, poking around under the kitchen counter. She returns to the table with some paper cups and a half-empty bottle, its label covered with cobwebs and dust.

"You can always trust a cowboy," Alice says, "to leave some drink for the next guy." She sits across from Mona and pours liquor into three cups, then looks over at me and shrugs. "Sorry, Hawke," she says. "You're fucked up enough."

Juniper looks at me with her doe eyes, then reaches for a cup.

"Mona?" Alice says. She lifts her eyes to Mona. Mona's hand slowly moves toward the paper cup. Her hand is a shadowed landscape under the sputtering light. The wick is sucking up the last of the kerosene from the bottom of the lantern. A mouse moves under the counter. Mona keeps her eyes on Alice, lifts the cup and drinks like she's got something to prove. Alice pours another shot for Mona, then sips her own like it's her first time. The flame dies and we are now lost from each other in the darkness.

"I know who you are," Alice says in her lowest smoke-ravaged voice. "You were the girl in the yellow dress."

The hollow sound of an empty paper cup dropping to the table. Mona, a dark hunched shadow, face in her hands. Outside the window, a sky blue with the last of the moonlight.

"Hawke busted your girlfriend and you paid a visit to the judge, didn't you?" Alice says.

The shadow of Mona does not move.

"The summer I worked as a janitor at the courthouse," Alice says. "I saw you go into his office in your cute little yellow dress. I got a bad feeling the next time I looked down that hall and there was the chief cop standing like a prison guard outside his Honor's door." Alice picks up the bottle and rights Mona's cup, pours in some more. "A bad, bad feeling," she says.

A small dark shadow crosses a shaft of moonlight on the open floor. The mouse is growing bold.

"I found something in that judge's garbage," Alice goes on.

Mona lifts her face from her hands and drinks more whiskey.

"A big white handkerchief," Alice says, "red with blood."

Mona props her hands on the table and pushes herself up. She tries to stand and falls back to the bench.

"It was embroidered with the letters CWB," Alice says. "The honorable Charles Winthrop Briggs."

"Don't," Mona whispers.

"You know what I found in that old *taibo*'s garbage, Hawke?" Alice says, looking over at me, her voice loud now, as if I were losing my hearing along with everything else. "A girl's blood, Hawke, a girl's wet blood."

"Why are you doing this?" Mona says.

Alice strikes a match, holds it to a cigarette in her mouth, leans her heavy breasts on the table, blows out the match. The tip of her cigarette burns bright and she blows smoke to the rafters.

"His Honor made me suck his cock," Alice says. "Or else

he'd see to it I got kicked out of nursing school."

Juniper's hand presses my knee, as if to say it's not my fault. And of course, it's not my fault, I've never touched a woman but when and where she wanted to be touched.

"I stayed off men for over a year after that," Alice says, "but then I wandered out under the stars with Hawke one night and remembered how much I used to enjoy a good ride."

Juniper takes her hand off my knee. "Such a healer," she says.

Mona's shadow stirs. "That dress," she says. "It was too short." She wags her head back and forth. "And yellow," she whispers.

Alice stubs out her smoke on the table. Shakes her head and keeps pouring whiskey.

"I didn't have anything but jeans to wear," Mona says in her flat voice. "I had to go to the Salvation Army to find something nice. I thought it was the kind of dress you could wear to church, or to an appointment with a judge. I thought if I wore something nice, he might be more inclined to..." She lifts the cup, pale in the dim moonlight, tips it to her mouth.

"*I* wasn't wearing no fucking yellow dress," Alice yells. She takes the whiskey bottle by its neck and throws it through the window, shattering the glass, freeing the room to the cold night air.

Mona's voice, as if nothing happened. "And then I thought maybe if I just let him do that to me, he'd change his mind," she says. "But Ruby went to prison anyway. She lost her kids." The white cup disappears inside Mona's fist. The room is still but for the sound of her crushing it. "You—" she says, and I hear the air catching inside her lungs, that familiar breaking sound before a woman begins to cry. "You were supposed to be a mountain man," she says. "You shaved off your beard. You cut your hair. You put on a suit and you never once looked at me in court." And here it comes. Yes, and now Mona is crying the way women do. And Juniper gets up and goes to Mona, and I shouldn't be here, this is a woman thing.

"It was supposed to be *him,*" Mona says. She slams the busted cup to the table. "My first time was supposed to be with a mountain man." She shakes off Juniper's hands, staggers to the door, and is gone.

***

The whispers of women. Cigarette smoke, the smell of coffee, the yip-yapping coyotes. Words whoosh in and out, the sea breaking inside my head. The whispers of women. *Diapers... no plumbing…get him out of this dump…place with a bathroom…any day now…vegetable...no, he won't… I'm telling you…hates doctors…needs prescriptions.*

Alice's coughing laugh, "Forget it! I'm not gonna steal drugs for no *taibo* narc."

Shhh…he's sleeping…not a narc…you know that!

Behind my tombstone eyelids, I put my two hands on the edge of the plank table, pull myself up from this wheelchair, give Alice and Juniper a look that will hold them in place. I then walk out naked and alone. In the freedom of the night I open my palm, starlight reflects off my perfect flake of obsidian. The coyotes fall silent, they wait on the ridge for this thing to be finished. They wait on prancing feet, yearning toward their next meal.

I'm suddenly out of my sweet dream and back in my wheelchair, my eyes flung open by a loud bang, bang, banging of metal against metal. Juniper and Alice are still sitting across from each other at the far end of the table, a candle burning between them.

"She's going crazy out there," Alice says on her way out the door.

"It must be Mona," Juniper says. "Alice will make her stop."

"Leave her alone," I say.

Outside the noise is getting stronger, louder. I imagine Mona out there, warming up like a batter at the plate, swinging a length of metal pipe against the empty water tank. Juniper moves the candle down to my end of the table as she scooches along the bench. "You know this is the first time Mona ever told anyone what happened?" she says.

The candle flame seems to bend under the weight of noise from the water tank.

"She lives in Alaska, all by herself out in the bush," Juniper says. "She only comes south to visit her parents in Arizona."

The banging is loud and steady. Mona's arms must be strong from splitting firewood.

"She has this thing about the bristlecones," Juniper says, "but the wind up there blew down her tent last night and the temperature dropped way below freezing, so she got this idea to come to the hot springs."

"If she's from Alaska," I say, "she should know how to handle the cold."

"Listen," Juniper says. "She stopped."

"Let her bang," I say. "She's breaking her silence."

Juniper combs her fingers roughly into her hair, holds her head between her hands and rubs her scalp.

"You knew, didn't you?" she says, her eyes closed. "You knew what that judge was doing to girls."

I turn my face to the four squares of starlight and broken glass framed by the window. It's dark now, the moon long gone. Did I know? Did Alice mention something that night on the reservation? Sunk into each other on a broken-spring sofa that someone hauled out into the sagebrush, out in the middle of nowhere, my teeth crashing into hers, that mouthful of crooked teeth. Crazy Alice, hot for sex one moment, pushing me off her the next, calling me a no-good cocksucking *taibo*.

The first birdcall comes from the marsh, and now the faintest touch of dawn outside the broken window.

"You know what I've never been able to figure out?" I say, my eye caught on a jagged point of window glass.

"Tell me," Juniper says.

"What comes first?" I say. "The morning light or the bird announcing the light."

Juniper sighs. I feel her moving beside me. I look and she's standing, her back to me. I lift my good arm and with one finger I trace the line of her spine through the soft doeskin of her dress.

"Drive me up into the mountains," I say, "as high as you can, and then please, for pity's sake, Juniper, please leave me."

Juniper says nothing, her back does not soften to my touch. I drop my hand to my lap. Four squares of jagged night fade into morning, and the marsh becomes obliviously alive with birds. And something else is happening outside. A discordant howling, an eerie amplification of sound. Juniper goes to the shattered window and looks out.

"Alice and Mona," she says. "They must be inside the water tank."

"You can drive away and have the jeep," I say. "I'll sign

you over the title." The women in the tank are cawing like crows, trying out every sound they can think of.

Juniper turns to face me. She gives me a look.

"What?" I say.

"I'm worried about your soul."

"This is about my body," I say. "This body's a junker. Take the jeep."

"I'm talking about if you kill yourself, how that will mess up your *soul,*" Juniper says.

"Jesus, Juniper," I say.

"I can't help it," she says. "That's how I feel."

Juniper is no more to me now than a dark shape framed by daybreak and cracked glass, impossible to reach. If only she would break a piece off, just one arrow point from the window, and give it into my one good hand. But the best Juniper can come up with is a hair brush. She stands behind and she brushes my hair. And the two in the tank, their voices are blending now, they're singing in harmony, not words, more female than words, females sounding off. They're raising some kind of a jeremiad from inside that empty tank and it's not me they're mourning. And Juniper softly braids my hair while the room fills with sunlight and the voices of wailing women plunge me deeper into whatever this thing is that I can't find my way out of.

***

My body sits propped against the root of a bristlecone, a root thick as a dragon leg and tougher than time. Dragon toes curl off over the edge of a white cliff. There are others around me, each separate and alone, some still standing after a few thousand years, some resting on the white gravel. This one leans into the abyss. I can't imagine better company for dying than these titans, but first I must be done with the last of the women. Right now I'm in the shadow of Alice's bulky form standing before me. She's wrapped in a wool blanket, her dark hair snaky against the sun. Hot sun, cold wind, everything is drastic at this elevation.

"Hypothermia's not the worst way to go," I say, just to move things along.

Alice bends and picks up a stick. "Nothing decomposes up here," she says. "First Man might've used this very stick to beat First Woman."

I lift my one good arm and pat the root behind me, point to a twisted branch that juts out like a sculpted gangplank. "I used to come here and stretch out on that," I say. "Maybe I'll snake myself out there." I look up at Alice and wink. "It's a great view," I say.

Alice tips her face to the clear blue sky. "Or if you'd rather stay put I could come by after the buzzards clean up the worst," she says. "Kick a few bones over the edge."

"That's sweet of you," I say.

"Which reminds me, I got you a present." From somewhere inside her blanket Alice pulls out a fifth of Southern Comfort. "My cousin Clarence John froze himself to death in a ditch by the highway," she says. "Didn't feel a thing." She cradles the bottle like a baby, then gives it into my one good hand. "You can out-Indian the Indians one last time," she says.

"Only if you unscrew the top for me," I say.

Alice breaks the seal and twists loose the cap. She sets the bottle on the white rocky soil within reach of my one good arm. Straightens up and looks down at me.

"Something I been meaning to ask you for years, Alice," I say.

"Last chance to ask," Alice says.

"Were you the one who shot me way back when?" I squint up into the plump darkness of her face.

Alice lets go into a fit of coughing laughter. "Your ego's just overblown enough you would think a thing like that," she says.

"You were so…" I'm losing words, my mind is scattering in the wind, it snags on the tip of a lightning-struck tree. Alice stands beneath the avenging sun, heavy and rooted, but back in her day she was all fire and crooked teeth.

"Keep asking around, Hawke," she says. "It wasn't me."

"Thanks for the whiskey, Alice."

She pulls her blanket tight. "You cleaned up nice, Hawke." She takes a last look beyond the edge, then heads for the jeep. She turns back once and yells, "For a cop."

I start to raise my voice to tell Alice she's okay, too, for a Paiute, but everything is too far gone for that kind of talk and here comes Mona. Mona only because Juniper choked at the last minute. She'd gone so far as to get me dressed in my skins, wheel me out to the jeep, help lift me into the passenger seat. She even strapped me in, but then she went off again about my soul and wouldn't get behind the wheel. So Alice climbed out the back seat with a groan and hoisted herself into the driver seat and floored it. My neck whipped back, but I managed to turn my head for a last look at Juniper jumping away from our dust, the doeskin dress I made her, morning sunlight green on the tips of her hair. Alice chased after Mona's rooster plume until we were blinded by it. She honked and tailgated until Mona pulled over and got out of her car and stomped back through the settling white cloud to see what we wanted. Alice said she needed a hand and Mona said sorry, she was on her way up to Alaska. Alice said I was too much for one woman, and

Mona looked north and said she had a long drive ahead of her. So I told her about this back way where no one but the scientists and the park rangers were allowed to go, an area unknown to tourists and vandals. I asked Mona to let me make good on my promise to take her to the bristlecones. And so she helped Alice carry me from the jeep, then wandered off. But now she's struggling back through the wind, her hands in the pockets of an orange down vest, navy watch cap pulled down over her ears. She stops in the shelter of my tree. She takes her hands from her vest pockets and touches her fingers to the rough tree scales, strokes her palms around a smooth round bulge that protrudes like a birthing from the scales. She kicks her heel into the pale gravel.

"There's no soil up here," she says. "The oldest living things on earth, and they've built themselves out of wind and stone."

She sits beside me, leans into the same root. "I had it in mind to see these bristlecones a couple of years ago," she says, "but my timing was off, the road was snowed under."

She's still got it, I can see that now, that just out-of-reach shimmering something that made me want her all those years ago. "My timing was off too," I say. We'd have done better if we'd met after I quit my job."

"All I had was some magazine article." Mona goes on like I hadn't spoken and maybe I didn't, maybe I'm already on my way. "It called them 'tortured,'" she says. "It called this 'a cruel existence.'" She lifts her arms, open to the world before us, breathes it in.

"Such nonsense," she says, "as if this can be turned into a story about people." She stands and digs into her pants pocket, then bends and carefully places a black rock on the white gravel next to the Southern Comfort. My perfect flake of obsidian.

"Mona," I say.

Mona stands straight. She looks into the wind. "That day in the courtroom," she says, "the bottom half of your face was white where you'd shaved off your beard. You'd cut your hair. You wore a suit. I'd never seen you in anything but jeans and buckskin." She looks down at me. "I was taking *birth* control pills for you," she says. And suddenly Mona is smiling. Mona is smiling and she squats easily down to my level, and I see how lithe and limber her body is, and her face is good to look at in a way that almost makes me wonder why I never bothered to take up with women my own age.

"I'm done with it now," Mona says, "done with the entire story."

And I gather my breath to ask Mona if she was the one, the one who shot me, but the air goes out of me empty. I've got no use for the question, no use for the answer. And now Mona is headed back for the jeep, her orange vest a bright spot against the colorless stones. The sound of an engine starting, then drifting away. Everything I need is now within my grasp. I'm so happy I could die.

SUSI KLARE

After raising a family in the temperate rainforest of Oregon's rugged and remote Coast Range, Susi Klare now resides on the dry side in Sisters. Many of her days are spent afoot, happily wandering the wild places of Central and Eastern Oregon.

LITERARY AWARDS & HONORS

Susi Klare is the recipient of a 2001 Oregon Literary Arts Fellowship and was awarded a month-long residency at Caldera Arts Center.

"As if Keeping it Secret" won First Place Fiction award in the Fifth Annual Peregrine Prize.

"At the Intersection of Heaven and Hell" was first place winner of the 2001 H.E. Francis Literary Competition, received a 2005 Pushcart Prize nomination by Fish Publishing, and was the runner-up in the *Mississippi Review* 2005 Prize.

"Blood and Roses" won the first place 2001 *Charter Oak Review* fiction prize under title "Wild Roses".

"The Salvation of My Soul" was awarded First Place 2003 *River City* Writing Award in Fiction.

"Naked Glass" was awarded second prize by Pulitzer Prize winner Robert Olen Butler in the 2003 Raymond Carver Short Story Award.

www.ingramcontent.com/pod-product-compliance
Lightning Source LLC
Chambersburg PA
CBHW050357190726
48284CB00007BB/2321

9781945587511